TRANSCENDENTAL MISCONCEPTIONS

R. D. Scott

BETA BOOKS • SAN DIEGO

Library of Congress Cataloging in Publication Data

Scott, R   D   1950-
    Transcendental Misconceptions

    Bibliography: p.
    Includes index.
    1. Transcendental Meditation.   I. Title.
BF637.T68S37   158   77-13503
ISBN 0-89293-031-4

Dedication

To my wife Susan, to my children, and
to lovers of truth everywhere.

NOTE FROM THE PUBLISHER

"If it looks like a duck, walks like a duck, and quacks like a duck, it must *be* a duck . . . though some may call it a golden-plumed peacock." This familiar farmyard metaphor could also stand as a thumbnail synopsis of the court's decision and opinon in the New Jersey TM case. On October 19, 1977, U.S. District Judge H. Curtis Meanor issued an extensive opinion holding that *the Transcendental Meditation (TM) movement of Maharishi Mahesh Yogi is religious in nature.* The opinion stated that the teaching of TM in New Jersey public schools is a violation of the First Amendment to the U.S. Constitution and is therefore prohibited. (The First Amendment requires the "separation of Church and State"; our courts have consistently interpreted this as a prohibition of government sponsorship or support of any form of religious teaching or practice.)

The Court's Opinion

Judge Meanor rendered his decision and written opinion upon the plaintiffs' motion for summary judgment. For that reason, the evidence which he considered in order to weigh the religious character of TM was limited to facts that were not disputed by either party to the action; it consisted essentially of the initiatory *puja*, the textbook used to teach the New Jersey courses, the deposition testimony of two TM initiators who actually taught classes in the Science of Creative Intelligence, plus the deposition and affidavit of defendant Jerry Jarvis, President of the TM movement in the United States.

The ruling and written opinion were given in response to plaintiffs' motion for summary judgment, filed on September 22, 1976. The motion in effect asked Judge Meanor to rule that TM is religious by legal definition. Such a motion, when granted, makes a trial unnecessary, since the only purpose of a trial is to resolve disputes over facts or evidence; if the facts are not disputed, a judge is qualified to weigh their meaning under the law without the aid of testimony. By his decision of October 19, Judge Meanor granted the motion for summary judgment, agreeing with plaintiffs that there was no real issue on any material fact, and that TM, its underlying philosophy, and its prayer of initiation, the *puja*, are religious as a matter of law. Summary judgments are notoriously difficult to obtain in Federal Court, even when the evidence seems conclusive. The fact that one was granted in this instance is an indication that the case against TM was truly "open and shut."

The final words of the Court are that:

"No inference was possible except that the teaching of SCI/TM and the *puja* are religious in nature. No other inference is 'permissible' or reasonable, especially because the court is dealing with the meaning of a constitutional term and not with a factual dispute . . .

"Although defendants have submitted well over 1500 pages of briefs, affidavits, and deposition testimony in opposing plaintiffs' motion for summary judgment, defendants have failed to raise the slightest doubt as to the facts or as to the religious nature of the teachings of the Science of Creative Intelligence and the *puja*. The teaching of the SCI/TM course in New Jersey public high schools violates the establishment clause of the first amendment, and its teaching must be enjoined."

This ruling is technically binding—as judicial precedent—only in New Jersey. Nevertheless, it is likely that other states and governmental agencies will calculate its meaning very carefully if they are considering endorsement of TM programs. In this way it becomes nearly as influential as if it were binding—or at least it does so to the extent to which people are made aware of its existence and content.

In the larger context of public policy, the decision itself and the strength of the Judge's language in describing TM's religious nature are expected to have a significant impact of Maharishi Mahesh Yogi's avowed strategy of using government and other public institutions as the primary missionary vehicle for Transcendental Meditation. For example, the SCI/TM organization is currently carrying on an aggressive campaign of seeking federal funds to support programs of teaching TM to prisoners in various state correctional institutions, which also falls under the First Amendment restrictions on government support of religion. As a direct result of this decision, it is likely that these and other doors now open to SCI/TM in its efforts to gain the use of taxpayers' money will be effectively closed.

excerpted by permission from *Spiritual Counterfeits Project Newsletter*, November, 1977, Vol. 3, No 6. © Spiritual Counterfeits Project, Inc. 1977. Further, and more detailed information may be obtained from Spiritual Counterfeits Project, Box 4308, Berkeley, Ca. 94704

INTRODUCTION

This is the story of my six years in the Transcendental Meditation movement and why I left it. I have attempted to tell a side of the TM® story that the public doesn't know—a side based on dishonesty and deception originating with Maharishi Mahesh Yogi himself and permeating the entire structure of TM® in its theory, practice and promotional organization.

What you will read in the following pages has never been told before. Much of it is based on secret documents available only to insiders. I was a successful full-time teacher of TM® and so came to learn this classified and suppressed information. In fact, for a time I actively participated in and supported both the deception of the general public and the dishonest practices of the movement.

An example of the gross deception and dishonesty perpetrated by the movement against both the public and its own members can be seen in this letter to the *Christian Science Monitor* of 7 July 1976:

> *The legal question of whether Transcendental Meditation (TM) is a religion or a non-religious meditation technique with educational and rehabilitative value is important.*
>
> *As a two-year TM meditator, I feel I must emphasize that TM is not a religion, worship or devotion. It is simply (yet profoundly) what 850,000 TM advocates say it is—a technique. Once the technique has been taught (which takes about 30 minutes) the meditator is on his own. The puja ceremony (a couple of minutes long) is simply a salute to the teachers who kept alive this old technique.*
>
> *TM works within the individual's own framework. Religion has not been added or subtracted. Yet some*

7

find their own religious beliefs strengthened, possibly because the mind and body settle into an extremely deep rest (metabolically catalogued as more restful than the state of deep sleep). This deep rest gives the usually chattering mind a chance to know itself, making TM a valuable self-help tool in rehabilitative and educational programs.

If self-knowledge is to be labeled "religion" then indeed TM must be labeled a "religious technique." And our schools and universities must also be labeled a part of "religion," for what is the pursuit of knowledge except ultimately to "know thyself?"

RW
California

I will show you how and why this letter is false and deceptive, even though the writer may be a perfectly sincere person who wholly believes what she has written to the public. Whether she knows it or not, Ms. Williams has been sadly duped by the TM® movement.

However, not everyone is being taken in. Through a series of unintentional discoveries, I was fortunate to have "the blinding darkness of ignorance removed by the application of the ointment of knowledge." After I left the movement, I found myself in a small but growing group of people who also felt that in spite of all the benefits offered by TM®, none was worth the price—one's very soul.

The intent of this book, then, is not malicious. Rather, it is an act of conscience—an attempt to tell the truth, to awaken the public to a great religious deception. It was the same spirit that led me, two years after I left the movement, to contact the Coalition for Religious Integrity, a national organization of concerned individuals and groups representing a broad spectrum of political, ideological and religious persuasions. The Coalition has joined with the Spiritual Counterfeit Project and with Americans United for Separation of Church and State to institute a lawsuit challenging TM®'s presence in the schools. The case will come to trial in New Jersey late this year. I will appear as an expert witness for the plaintiffs who charge that TM® is not secular but rather is subtly-disguised Hinduism, and as such is in violation of the Constitutional principle of separation of church and state.

What is the basis for this case? There is a lot of legal terminology in the complaint filed in the United States District Court, District of New Jersey, and technically referred to as Civil Action No. 76-341. But in essence the prosecution maintains that:

1. TM® is a religion and a religious practice—specifically, Hinduism.

2. As such, it has no place in the public schools because the First Amendment of the U.S. Constitution requires the strict and complete separation of church and state. That means separation between any and all religious organizations on the one hand and the secular governments (local, state and national) of our country on the other.

3. But in four New Jersey public school systems, TM® has been introduced and supported by public tax money. This clearly violates the First Amendment.

4. Therefore the court should decide in favor of the plaintiffs and should pass judgment against the defendants, which permanently prohibits TM® from being taught in the public schools.

To repeat, then, this is my sincere attempt to bring the truth to the public about this religious deception and secret attack on the Constitution. I hope also that people will base their decision about whether or not to become involved in TM® on *all* the facts, not just the selected "facts" that the TM® movement wants the public to hear. As Jesus teaches us in the Bible (John 8:32), "And you will know the truth, and the truth will set you free."

Chapter ONE

MY SEARCH FOR SELF:
GETTING INTO TM®

The Transcendental Meditation movement claims that the technique of TM® is the ultimate solution to all problems facing humanity. Maharishi Mahesh Yogi, the founder of TM®, and his followers claim that it offers people the use of one hundred percent of their mental potential. They also say that TM® brings excellent health and "naturally correct" social behavior. In addition, they declare, the natural result of this improved social behavior will ultimately be world peace. Last, they adamantly maintain that the technique of TM® is not religious. These reasons should be enough to convince any reasonable person that TM® is worth learning.

At least, that's how I looked at it in 1968 when I was initiated into TM®. I was a perfect target for the TM® public relations pitch. I had just turned eighteen, was the product of an upper middle class suburban Connecticut community, achieved well in high school, actively participated in the life of the local Congregational church, and had been involved in movements such as the National Association for the Advancement of Colored People

(NAACP), Congress of Racial Equality (CORE) and the New England Committee for Non-Violent Action (CNVA). These groups had all been very active in the 1960's attempting to create a more harmonious, peaceful and fulfilled world through the honest-hearted efforts of their members.

Those were my goals then and they continue today. They're a large part of my reasons for writing this book. They also were the reasons I found myself, on a warm April day that year, heading to the Midtown Motor Inn in New Haven.

The Appointment

I had an appointment to keep, and although I felt somewhat self-conscious carrying half a dozen carnations, I was also quite excited. I arrived at the Inn and opened the door to the lobby. As the door closed behind me, the street sounds were instantly hushed. There was a man checking out at the counter, and I noticed how quiet the lobby was. Before I had a chance to speak, the receptionist pointed to the elevator and told me I wanted the second floor. "Must be the flowers," I thought.

As I entered the elevator, I made a quick mental doublecheck of my supplies: six carnations, an apple, an orange, a fresh white handkerchief and $35 in cash. I was ready for the experience of my life. My finger pressed the second-floor button and the doors slid quietly together.

I had been briefed at a talk the night before, along with 250 other attendees, that we might have a short wait before our individual appointments due to the large number of people taking the course. The Beatles had recently created a lot of publicity for TM® as a result of their involvement with Maharishi. Therefore I wasn't surprised to find the waiting room packed with people, baskets full of fruit, flowers and handkerchiefs, and an air of hushed excitement. Every few minutes someone would be ushered in or out of the room by shoeless attendants. I couldn't help wondering who had already been initiated and who hadn't.

A soft-spoken girl asked me to have a seat. She asked my name and then went across the room to a desk in the corner. She returned momentarily and told me to wait because they were slightly behind schedule. People continued to come and go. I noticed a strong smell of incense issuing from somewhere nearby. It was very pleasant smelling, not overpowering. The girl returned and asked me if I had my money. I gave her the $35. She came back with a receipt which stated that the payment was for "personal instruction." Finally, after a wait of almost half an hour, the nameless girl quietly asked me to remove my shoes and to hold a basket which contained the carnations, fruit, handkerchief and an interview form which I had filled out the previous night.

"It must be my turn," I figured. And indeed it was. The door opened and in walked my initiator, a blonde woman in her late twenties with stockinged feet and a radiant smile. She approached me and asked me to go with her. We left the waiting room and headed down the hotel corridor. A few doors down, the smell of incense was much stronger. She stopped at a door and quietly opened it. I followed her in and she closed the door behind me. It was very dark. The air was thick with a haze of incense and curtains were drawn. As my eyes adjusted to the light, I could see a lighted candle on a table against the wall.

It was a hotel room with the usual hotel room furnishing—two double beds and a night table. However, the room decor was far from typical. There was a table draped with a large white sheet upon which was sitting the burning candle, along with an assortment of brass artifacts and a picture of an elderly Indian man whom I later learned was Guru Dev, Maharishi's teacher, amid a forested scene. The picture was leaning against the wall. Centered on the table and directly in front of the picture was a shiny brass plate. A brass candleholder supported a lighted candle on the right side of the picture. It was an unusual picture. There was something strange about the man's eyes. On the other side of the picture was an incense holder with two sticks of burning incense, giving off the same delightful fragrance I had noticed in the waiting room. The smoke rose straight up from each of the sticks in thin, unwavering lines. The air was very still. In addition, there were three small brass dishes lined up in front of the brass plate. One contained rice, one contained water, and the third, a light brown powder. Another unusual brass piece held what appeared to be a small white chunk of a moth ball.

[The significance of all this paraphernalia wasn't explained to me at the time. Nowadays it is mentioned briefly to initiates, but the truth about it isn't told. I can tell you, however, that the draped table was in fact an altar, and that what followed was a religious ceremony. But much more about that later.]

To return: my initiator, whose name was Marilyn, motioned for me to sit in one of the two chairs facing the altar. She sat in the other. She took the basket from me and placed it on the left side of the altar. Then she took the interview form, glanced at it and dropped it to the floor beside her chair. She turned to me and said that it was very important that I never tell anyone, ever, about what was to take place. She asked me if I would maintain complete secrecy about the experience.

It was obvious that the show would go no further without an affirmative reply from me. I was committed. I had paid my money and come this far. I wanted to see the whole show. So I agreed to the condition with a quiet, "Yes." Obviously, I am now breaking my promise. I fully admit that. I have my reasons, which I'll explain fully later.

Marilyn leaned toward me and told me in a whisper that she would perform a brief ceremony which I should observe, and we would then get on with the initiation. She stood up and beckoned me to stand next to her. Taking the carnations in her left hand, she removed one from the bunch and with her right hand dipped it into the dish of water. Then she sprinkled droplets of water on the brass plate and surrounding areas and began "mumbling."

That is, the sounds from her mouth were barely audible. It was difficult to understand what she was saying. I was slightly familiar with French and Spanish, but the words she was speaking were not from those languages; this language

14

was altogether foreign to me. A few months later I learned that she had been speaking in Sanskrit. And two years later I was to learn the exact ceremony she performed, word for word, movement for movement. This ceremony is called the *puja,* which is Sanskrit for "worship." The English translation of it, given in the appendices, may be a shock to anyone who has been taken in by the TM® claims, as I was at first, that TM® is strictly secular.

Marilyn's mumbling grew into a chant, the chant into a song. She placed the handkerchief, the fruit, more flowers, more water, rice and brown powder on the tray while she sang. She took a stick of incense and placed it in the candle flame until the incense burst into flame itself. With this she lit the piece of moth ball—which was actually a piece of camphor—and with the flaming holder drew imaginary circles in the air before the picture of the ancient Indian, Guru Dev.

Much as I tried to pretend at being at ease, I felt very out of place, uncomfortable, "spooked." Luckily I wasn't required to speak, because I would have found it very difficult. If her intent was to throw me off guard, she had succeeded completely.

The climax of the ceremony arrived when she said something that sounded like "clambake" and placed the last few flowers on the tray. Then, with a sweeping downward motion of the arms, she knelt before the altar, her palms together, inviting me to kneel with her.

Even at that stage of my naivete, this seemed an overtly religious act, though we had been told at the talk that there was nothing religious about the TM® technique. We had been carefully assured that the instruction would in no way conflict with anyone's religious beliefs. Who was I to question the integrity of these people? They had claimed that their program was going to create naturally right social behavior in those who practiced the technique. They had appealed to my idealism and had talked glowingly about human betterment. It didn't make sense then that deception and dishonesty should play any part in the marketing of such a technique. In my inexperienced condition, I was

15

forced to conclude that this display was not religious in nature. And leaving logic aside, it was impossible to judge, since I hadn't understood a single word of the song she had sung.

It seemed she was waiting for me to join her on the floor. You can guess what I did. There I was, kneeling awkwardly next to her. Never before had I felt so incredibly uncomfortable and out of place.

I Receive My Mantra

After a prolonged silence, with the two of us kneeling together on the hotel room floor in a worshipful pose before Guru Dev, Marilyn began mumbling again. This time, however, I found she was repeating one word over and over. At first it was nothing more than the beginnings of a whisper. She increased her repetition in volume and clarity as she continued until I could distinguish a specific pronunciation.

"This," I thought, "must be my mantra. My very personal and unique meaningless sound. This sound will do great things for me. It will take me to quieter levels of thinking and ultimately to my innermost self, to bliss-consciousness."

Marilyn was deeply absorbed in her chanting. I noticed her eyes. They were intense. They were imploring me to do something. She began making circular motions with her left hand and nodded her head at me, up and down, up and down.

Suddenly I realized I was being asked, although in a rather peculiar manner, to imitate her. I listened to her pronunciation a few more times and then gave it a try. *"Ong . . . Ong . . . Ong . . ."* I could tell from Marilyn's expression that I didn't quite have it right. Still, she said nothing. She simply continued repeating the sound, though somewhat slower and more emphatically. I noticed my mistake immediately and began again. *"Ah-ing . . . Ah-ing . . . Ah-ing . . . Ah-ing . . ."* Marilyn's radiant smile returned to her face, and she indicated with more circular motions of her hands that I was on the right track and should continue. I was apparently doing OK. I began to feel a little more comfortable. At least now we seemed to have something in common.

The tension continued to subside as we proceeded with our chanting duet. After a few more moments on the floor, Marilyn arose and sat down in her chair, indicating with a gesture that I should do the same. Our chanting continued and she said, "Now close the eyes." No sooner said than done, although I had no idea what to expect. Marilyn had stopped chanting and I could hear myself chanting alone, *"Ah-ing . . . Ah-ing . . . Ah-ing . . ."*

Marilyn's soft voice broke in. "More quietly," she said. I lowered my volume and continued. *"Ah-ing . . . Ah-ing . . ."* Again Marilyn quietly interrupted with, "Still more quietly." My anticipation was growing, second by second. When would I experience that promised bliss? I reduced my volume once again as Marilyn instructed and found that I couldn't speak any more softly without whispering. From a whisper, Marilyn led me to even softer repetitions until it was a chore to continue aloud.

After treading that fine line between the barely audible whisper and complete silence for a few more repetitions, Marilyn broke in. "Now, just think it."

What a relief! At first I maintained the same speed and regularity in my mental repetitions as when I had been repeating it aloud. But very quickly, in ten to fifteen seconds, the mantra seemed to come alive of its own accord. It lengthened, slowed down and then became softer. I was fascinated and deeply absorbed in its delicate mental ballet. Remarkable!

"Now, open the eyes," Marilyn whispered. Why did she want me to do that? After I opened them, she asked me if *it* was easy. I wasn't sure *what* was supposed to be easy, but nothing seemed to be difficult, so I said, "Yes." Then it was time to close my eyes again and continue thinking the mantra over and over easily and, as the TM® teachers are trained to say, innocently.

I began to think it, *"Ah-ing . . . Ah-ing . . . Ah-ing . . .,"* waiting for the mental ballet to begin. But this time nothing happened. I began to think, "Come on, mantra. Do your thing . . . Maybe I'm trying too hard . . . Perhaps I should try it more quickly . . . or more slowly." I heard Marilyn take a deep breath and began wondering what she was doing. I thought about the altar and the picture of the old man, the room, and about why nothing seemed to be happening. Then I realized that I wasn't thinking the mantra. Immediately I started thinking it over and over. It faded away, and again I was absorbed in more thoughts about what was supposed to happen and why nothing seemed to be happening.

Suddenly I was jolted back to my senses by Marilyn's voice. "Now, again, open the eyes," she whispered.

I thought to myself, "What is this all about? Open the eyes, close the eyes, open the eyes, close the eyes. What a bunch of nonsense!"

After my eyes were opened, Marilyn asked me if I had experienced any thoughts. Yes, of course I had. She assured me that was OK and that I should just easily return to the mantra repetition whenever I realized I was thinking other thoughts. She was concerned about whether it was easy again, and as far as I could tell there was still nothing difficult, so my answer remained "Yes."

Then she asked if I had felt some relaxation. That was an interesting question. I had been waiting for a bolt of lightning to flash through my brain, and I had completely overlooked the fact that I was quite relaxed physically. My mental experience to that point had been nothing more than the normal daydream, much like when the mind drifts off in the middle of listening to someone's conversation—if that person asks for your thoughts on what he said, you suddenly have the embarrassing realization that you didn't hear the last half of the story.

The only obvious difference, aside from the mantra, between normal daydreaming and this experience of daydreaming seemed to be that since I was anticipating a flashy mental experience, I was very aware of my mental activity and therefore had a chance to "look in" on a daydream rather than to be absorbed in it.

Marilyn seemed to approve of my results to that point and instructed me to close my eyes and continue mentally. It seemed as though five minutes went by, during which time I was thinking my mantra, pursuing thoughts, wondering if I was doing OK, having realizations that I wasn't thinking the mantra, and then restarting my mental repetition of it. During all of this, I was feeling some relaxation.

"Now, open the eyes . . . slowly," Marilyn quietly instructed. I took my time and finally my eyes were open, staring at the altar. The brass plate was piled high with the fruit and flowers, and the candle and the incense were still burning, filling the room with flickering light and perfume-scented smoke. I turned my head toward Marilyn and saw that she, too, was staring at the altar. How long had we been together in the room? I glanced at my watch. It had been a little less than twenty minutes.

Marilyn adjusted her position in the chair and turned toward me. She opened the conversation with more questions. "Was it easy? Did you feel some quietness? Some relaxation?" She was concerned about whether I had found the mantra disappearing much. I told her it had happened a few times but that I had returned to the mantra whenever I realized it was gone. She said, "This is what we do. We don't try to hold on to the mantra or try to push it away. We just think it easily and effortlessly, and when we realize that we aren't thinking the mantra, we just effortlessly begin it again. This is Transcendental Meditation."

So that was TM®!

Marilyn continued, "I'm going to take you across the hall now and you'll meditate on your own for ten to fifteen minutes. Someone will come for you. When they do, take a few minutes to come out slowly before you open the eyes. Then you'll go back to the waiting room and we'll have another brief meeting together."

After she took me across the hall, I sat down in a comfortable arm chair, closed my eyes and began meditating. Time passed. The door opened and a soft voice told me to come out slowly. It was another shoeless attendant. She took me back to the waiting room and asked me to fill out a questionnaire about my experience. Most of the questions had already been asked by Marilyn during the initiation. Marilyn returned and we walked back down to the room with the altar. She asked me the same sort of questions as before, reviewed the form with my answers, and told me there would be a meeting the following evening with all the people who had been instructed that day.

She told me to meditate that evening before dinner for half an hour, again in the morning before breakfast for half an hour, and once more before dinner the next day. The meeting would be at 8 p.m. in the same hall in downtown New Haven where we had heard our preparatory lecture. "Any questions?" she asked, her face beaming. "None at the moment," I answered. She said it was traditional for the teacher to return a piece of fruit, a flower and the handkerchief to the new meditator. This she did and then showed me to the door.

I never saw her again. She wasn't at the follow-up meetings, and to this day I have learned nothing more about her.

I walked down the hall, my mind full of unformulated questions, my hands full of the remains of that strange ceremony. It would be more than two years before I witnessed the puja again. But the next time it would be Maharishi Mahesh Yogi himself doing the honors.

Chapter Two

ENLIGHTENMENT, INC.:
HOW I BECAME A TM® TEACHER

The first step on the road to becoming a TM® teacher is a very obvious one: become a TM® meditator. Once a meditator, the promotions begin and continue almost as quickly as one desires.

A Vision of Possibilities

I felt that being initiated was a giant step into an exciting new world. I had received my secret mantra. I knew how to use it to help me relax and thereby tap more of my inner resources, and during the three follow-up sessions after my personal initiation, a vision of possibilities was described that sounded "out of this world."

We were told that by meditating regularly twice a day and maintaining a healthy schedule of activity between meditations, we would develop to a level of cosmic consciousness. This would happen automatically—without any effort at all! My understanding of what was meant by "cosmic consciousness" at that time left much to the imagination. I was unfamiliar with the concept but was highly intrigued by the term. It certainly sounded impressive, and yet the TM® teacher claimed that as impressive as it might sound, we shouldn't think of it as anything special. We should consider it as just living a normal life. However, any experience of life prior to gaining CC (the movement's widely-used abbreviation for cosmic consciousness) was to be considered subnormal, less than mediocre.

It was a most effective way to get our curiosity glands functioning. How could we *not* think of CC as "something special" after a build-up like that? It's nothing special, he says, just normal life. Then we think to ourselves, "Well, aren't we living a *normal* life now?" And then we learn that what *he* meant by normal life was CC; he didn't mean normal life in the commonly accepted sense. Now we all had a new definition of normal; if we accepted it, we had no alternative but to meditate until we achieved CC. Otherwise we would be denying ourselves the experience of a full *normal* life.

I don't mean to imply that I blindly assented to all the information taught during those follow-up meetings (at least I did not then). The notion of CC was intriguing, but it also seemed more like remote theory than a real possibility. There was no denying that TM® was a powerful means to relax. I also noticed an energy boost after meditating, and I did experience some increased clarity of mind during the day. These were the symptoms of correct meditation, we were told. Regular meditation would compound these benefits automatically, much like the daily compounding of interest on the balance in a savings account. So we could expect to find eventually that we would experience the same quiet relaxation which we gained through meditation even in the midst of the most vigorous and exhausting activity. When that "momentum of silence" carried itself through the full 24 hours of the day, we would know we had attained that "normal" condition of cosmic consciousness. "Doing less and accomplishing more," the expression went. No longer would we feel the pressures of a tiring day. Suffering, as we knew it, would for all practical purposes no longer exist. Our "self" would be separate from activity, and we would function as it "witnesses" to all spatial and temporal "relative" experience. We would be permanently grounded in the non-changing field of the "Absolute," a field of "Being," and yet we would continue to cycle through the waking, dreaming and sleeping states of consciousness as before. The difference would lie in our perceptions. If someone were to observe us before CC and after CC, they would see no apparent change, we were told.

It sounded fascinating, yet somewhat far-fetched. What difference did it make anyway? Whether I believed all that philosophical mumbo-jumbo or not, the technique certainly seemed to have its real down-to-earth benefits.

During one of the follow-up meetings we were asked by the teacher if we had noticed any experience of "no thoughts and no mantra." We were told that the most common time during meditation when we might have such an experience would be immediately after the mantra had slipped away during our mental repetition of it and before becoming absorbed in the meditation-daydreaming I described as experiencing during my first meditation. There were quite a few hands in the air to respond to the teacher's question.

That, we were told, is transcending—the fourth major state of consciousness. Hence, the name Transcendental Meditation. Meditation refers to thinking, generally a contemplative type of thinking. Transcendental means to be beyond. Therefore, Transcendental Meditation takes you beyond the field of thinking and lets your awareness settle to the "source of thought," that silent field of "Being" which supposedly forms the basis of all activity.

The fact that we had experienced these moments of blank mind was given as evidence of the possibility of developing CC. If we were capable of having even brief glimpses of Transcendental Consciousness (TC) during meditation so early in our practice of the technique, then it was only logical to conclude, according to the teacher, that by gaining greater familiarity with it through regular meditation we would ultimately be able to maintain a conscious experience of that "ground" state of the source of thought beneath the "field" of any sense perceptions or activity. That would be the fifth state of consciousness, otherwise known as Cosmic Consciousness or CC. A 24-hour-a-day inner wakefulness, even when we were asleep!

TM® was beginning to seem like a metaphorical iceberg. There was more beneath the surface than one would ever imagine from a cursory examination of the introductory claims.

Finally, in further support of the natural development to CC which was being promised, the teacher provided us with an additional explanation of why we could reasonably expect to find ourselves in that glorious state of unbounded freedom of CC before too long. As a matter of fact, at that time it was stated that it would be possible for an average individual to attain CC within five to seven years of regular meditation.

The teacher pointed out that when we were meditating, we were experiencing very deep and quiet levels of thinking. Corresponding to those quiet levels of thinking were quieter levels of functioning of the physical activity of the body and the nervous system. As a result of gaining that deep rest, deep-rooted stresses in the body and the nervous system were loosened up and had a chance to be removed by the natural tendency of the body to eliminate any restrictions to its normal functioning. In this way, we were told, the body, through the elimination of stresses, would very quickly "normalize" itself. Then the normally-functioning body and nervous system would provide the basis for the field of Transcendental Consciousness to express itself fully in all our perceptions and actions. Once again, the end result of CC was the promise.

My experience told me that deep rest did accompany the TM® experience. And it seemed to make sense that stress is less when you're feeling well-rested. But, once again, what difference did it make whether it all led to CC or not? I knew that TM® made me feel good, and that was enough for me, at least for the time being.

The Enlightenment Factory in the Early Days

The TM® movement was relatively small at that time,

not that the course I attended was small. By current standards it was huge—250 initiated in one weekend in one course! That would be considered incredible today. Back in 1968, there were few initiators. It wasn't until 1970 that Maharishi began putting all of his efforts into the manufacture of thousands of "little Maharishis." Because of the lack of initiators, a course was offered in New Haven only once every few months. If someone wanted to travel to New York, there were more frequent courses, but the inconvenience of having to commute back and forth for four days in a row eliminated that as a possibility for most.

In addition to the infrequent initiation courses, there was also little opportunity for adequate "checking," as the follow-up procedure was called. The main coordination for the TM® movement in the New Haven area was handled by a small group of students at Yale University who had been meditating for a relatively short time. Whenever a teacher arrived in town to give an introductory course, he or she would spend as much time as possible with meditators in the area. The meditators were encouraged to help with publicity for upcoming courses, to begin learning how to give introductory talks, and to train to become "checkers" by learning the checking notes. The checking procedure is a programmed set of instructions designed to take a meditator through the correct procedures for starting meditation properly. It is dictated to the meditator-in-training by the teacher and learned by rote. It is repeated identically word for word each time a person is "checked," no matter how many times an individual may have been through the process. It is considered by most initiators to be the perfect TM® de-bugger and is in fact fairly effective in clearing up most questions meditators may develop about the more obvious mechanics of the technique, such as what to do about excessive thoughts other than the mantra, how to deal with uncomfortable sensations that may develop during meditation, and other technical questions.

The checking procedure, however, will not answer a meditator's questions about whether he has the right mantra, or how his mantra was chosen. These were very common questions in those days and continue to be so today. Whenever the topic came up, I never once heard a straightforward reply to either of those questions. That information was apparently reserved for the initiators only.

The teacher training courses that were available between 1968 and 1970 were held in Rishikesh, India, where Maharishi's ashram overlooked the Ganges River. The cost of travel to attend one of these courses was prohibitive for many people. Why not hold them in the U.S.? I learned a few years later that Maharishi wanted to hold the courses in Rishikesh because of the presence of the many highly evolved souls of departed Indian saints, yogis, and spiritual masters in that region of the Ganges River Valley. That seems far from a secular concern!

Another reason the courses were relatively small compared with teacher training courses of today (where as many as 2000 people may attend) was the fact that the age restrictions and educational prerequisites were much more limiting than they are today. A minimum of four years of college was required, and I believe the minimum age was 21.

So the enlightenment corporation was definitely operational. There was a home office and factory in Rishikesh, with capabilities of manufacturing a limited number of meditation guides. There was the product, TM®. [It had no patent on it in those days and was therefore in the public domain. Today the trademark "TM®" is legally owned by the movement. A fair amount of work had gone into the research and development of a marketable package for the product.] There was a small core of dedicated non-profit distributors who retail-marketed the technique after the fashion of the traveling medicine man (and those distributors weren't afraid to return to the same town twice!).

So I purchased my own stock of "Dr. Maharishi's Bottled Bliss" with just the right prescription for my daily dosage, and I spent the next year-and-a-half working my way to the bottom of that first big bottle.

The Manufacturing Facilities Move West

Eric, a good friend who was more involved in the activities offered by the Students International Meditation Society (or SIMS, as one group of the TM® movement was commonly known), had occasionally suggested that I attend a residence course. This can best be compared to a weekend retreat, although the TM® people prefer to call them weekend "advances."

At a residence course, a group of meditators spends time doing extra meditations, performing yoga exercises and listening to tapes of Maharishi discussing TM® and higher states of consciousness. The purpose of these courses is to speed up the elimination of "stress" through the additional rest gained from the extra meditations.

The courses were generally held in hotels or off-season resort facilities during holiday periods or occasionally during a long weekend. Jerry Jarvis, the national director of SIMS, occasionally would serve as moderator at these residence courses. Eric had attended one of these at the Holiday Inn in Meriden, Connecticut. He was very impressed with Jerry Jarvis and also with the results of the weekend experience.

I never felt I had the money or time to spare, and so I never attended any of them. However, in January, 1970, Eric mentioned that there was going to be a course that summer in Poland Spring, Maine. Maharishi himself would be present for 30 days to give advanced instruction in TM®. It would be like one long incredible residence course! He said he was planning to attend and he encouraged me to go, too. I thought about it for a few days and finally decided to join him.

I worked during the spring and saved up the $375 to pay for the course, which began sometime near the middle of June. I rode with a group of other meditators from the New Haven area up to Poland Spring.

As we neared Poland Spring, a few people in the car who had previously attended other residence courses commented about how peaceful the atmosphere was. I couldn't help but agree. The woods of Maine were a paradise compared to the noise of the city back home in New Haven. But apparently the peacefulness they were referring to was much more subtle than I had realized. "We must be getting near to Maharishi," they said. The rather contagious attitude began to develop that this was to be an extremely esoteric experience. Very few people would ever be fortunate enough to have this opportunity!

We finally arrived and headed toward the hotel lobby for registration. We all received I.D. badges, were assigned rooms, and were given a schedule of activities for the rest of the day. That old hotel was quite a place. It used to be a famous New England resort but apparently had been out of use for many years. It was elegant, but it had seen better days. The hotel was famous for the mineral springs on the property. People used to travel from all over the world for the medicinal benefits attributed to those springs—and Poland Spring bottled water is still available in some specialty shops around the country. In more recent years the hotel had served as a rehabilitation and work camp for teenagers. In addition it had been used occasionally for large group outings and picnics. The hotel sat in the middle of the Poland Spring golf course, which was also still in use.

The rooms had just been repainted by Maharishi's people to dress them up a bit. I later met a fellow from California who had come a few weeks early to help do some of the refurbishing.

So we registered, meditated, had dinner and then went to the grand ballroom to await Maharishi's arrival.

The entire hall was filled with rows of folding chairs; at the front of the hall was a stage. On the stage was a platform with a gold sofa. An easel standing behind the sofa held a picture of Guru Dev, the same picture I had seen two years earlier at my initiation. On either side of the platform were rows of chairs filled with well-dressed, neatly-groomed men and women. These were all teachers of TM® and other close followers of Maharishi. Shortly, the entire hall was filled with about 1,200 other meditators like me. We were all wearing our "Sunday best." It had been stated in the pre-course bulletins that jackets and ties would be in order for the evening meeting for men, dresses for the ladies. This was so we would all be in keeping with the "dignity" surrounding Maharishi.

Maharishi was announced, and as he walked into the room, I was amazed by his size. He was tiny! The initiators prayerfully placed their hands together and bowed their heads as Maharishi passed them. Many offered him flowers as he walked by on his way to the sofa. He accepted the flowers and then placed them on the table in front of the sofa. He sat down on a deerskin which Jerry Jarvis had placed on the sofa before Maharishi had come in [a deerskin is traditional for yogis to sit on]. Maharishi sat quietly; he took his time examining the crowd. His smile was radiant. He then began speaking softly into the microphone. There was a hush throughout the crowd when he began talking—we all listened silently.

As he spoke, he played with the flowers on the table. He opened by telling us how happy he was to see so many meditators together for the purpose of gaining knowledge of the truth of life. He explained that he had come to the United States because it was such a creative country, such a progressive country, that the thrust of life was creative and progressive. Therefore he felt that a country with those qualities would be more apt to listen to his teachings. India, his homeland, was too steeped in traditions of ignorance, and he figured that since the teaching was so practical, if reasonable people heard it they would put it into practice. He complimented us on our desire to become "knowers of reality," as he put it.

He spent three hours outlining his objectives for our one month together with him. And he emphasized the point that we *would* be, without a doubt, knowers of reality before the month was out. He told us the schedule for the month. It was going to be incredibly busy, although there would be opportunities for extra meditations during the middle of the course. The combination of gaining a deeper experience of meditation combined with a deeper understanding of our experience would produce profound changes in our level of consciousness, he promised. He ended that first evening by telling us to get some sleep and that we would all meet again in the morning.

The next morning Maharishi described the process of "rounding" which we would use when we started doing extra meditations. "Rounding" is the combination of performing a series of special yoga postures, known as asanas, followed by five minutes of a special yoga breathing exercise, known as pranayama, after which we would close our eyes, sitting in our comfortable meditation chair or on the bed, and begin to meditate. We were instructed to meditate our normal length of time and then, after taking two to three minutes to come slowly out of meditation, we should finish with five more minutes of pranayama. That would complete one "round." Maharishi emphasized that it was very important to stick very closely to the rounding schedule which he would be providing because there was a potential negative side-effect of too much deep rest too quickly, known as "heavy unstressing." An individual could conceivably experience such radical changes in his perceptions that he or she might incur severe negative emotional reactions to the experience.

According to Maharishi, stress is stored in our nervous systems as the result of sensory overloads. These overloads can be compared to tightly crumpled balls of cellophane which are stuffed into a box. As the crumpled balls accumulate, they become a permanent fixture within the box and leave little or no room for any other use of the box. This box full of crumpled cellophane is comparable to the TM® movement's view of the majority of nervous systems full of stresses. Gaining rest during TM® is comparable to opening the lid on the box. The release of stress can therefore be compared to the balls of cellophane uncrumpling themselves. If too many balls loosen up too quickly, the result will be a radically changed interior space which

30

would require a sudden reorientation for any constituents of the box to maintain or achieve stability.

With that understanding of the nervous system we are expected to believe that if too many stresses are released too quickly as a result of the supposedly incredibly deep rest gained from rounding, then the emotional, physical and psychological reorientation that would be required of the meditator would be too much to handle comfortably. This concept of stress is only hypothetical—thus far there is no evidence to support the notion of stress and release of stress. Supposedly, this process of rounding was designed to smooth out the rapid release of stress due to the increased depth of rest which the nervous system was experiencing.

We did begin a limited program of rounding in the next few days. The maximum number of rounds which Maharishi authorized us to do during the middle of the course was six or eight. A round took me about 50 minutes, so I spent almost seven hours rounding for a couple of days during the middle of the course. This was my very first contact with "long meditating," and I found it extremely mellow. I felt very "floaty" by the end of the course. During most of the course we did two rounds in the morning and two rounds in the evening. Maharishi programmed the rounding so that by the time the course was over, we were all back to our regular one meditation in the morning and one in the evening.

There were quite a few evenings set aside for questions about experiences during rounding. Maharishi would humorously deal with most questions and made everyone feel comfortable that as long as our meditations went "easily," we had nothing to worry about. He encouraged us by saying that we were evolving very quickly. He spent one evening explaining the development of the seven states of consciousness. It brought back memories of the first three days of my TM® experience when I had learned about CC. Now it developed that there were stages beyond even the fifth state of consciousness! Would it ever end? Apparently it would. But not until we reached the seventh state of consciousness, which Maharishi called Unity Consciousness. We were led to believe, although it was never stated outright by either Maharishi or Jerry Jarvis, that Maharishi was in that glorious state of total enlightenment which permitted an awareness of complete at-one-ness with the entire universe.

What a promise! What would be required to get to this UC, as Maharishi called it? Just regular meditation? Yes, we were told that if we wanted to speed up the process, advanced techniques would be available as we progressed in our personal evolution of consciousness. And the quickest way to reach the highest state of consciousness would be to become a teacher of TM®. The general consensus at that point was, "Well, Maharishi, just point us in the right direction and let's get on with it!"

Between CC and UC was a sixth state of consciousness called God Consciousness (GC), which was supposed to be very flashy. In GC it would be possible to see the molecular level of creation, auras, and other subtle phenomena at that level. Now referred to by the movement as "refined CC," GC was alluring, but not nearly so enticing as Unity.

Other lecture topics which Maharishi covered during our many meetings with him were angels and the celestial realm and "dropping the body" before and after CC (i.e., what happens when a person dies before gaining enlightment and how that is different from the experience of death for one who has attained Cosmic Consciousness). Maharishi also spoke of his life with Guru Dev, maya (the unreality of the deceptive world of relativity and change, the only truth being the non-changing absolute field of Being which never changes), the three gunas (an understanding from the *Bhagavad-Gita,* a Hindu religious document, about how relative creation operates), the importance of devotion to develop from CC to GC, and hours and hours of lectures about the Absolute Non-Changing Field of Being, the Relative Ever-Changing Field of Activity, and the importance of bringing the absolute into the relative. After some prodding, he discussed his views on marriage. He felt it was a waste of time that could otherwise be devoted to "spiritual development." He strongly advocated celibacy.

While we were learning all of this tremendously esoteric and profound knowledge, we were also learning to give first introductory lectures. It was curious to note that virtually none of the material which was being covered by Maharishi during this one-month course was contained in the introductory lecture material. As a matter of fact, the most controversial claim made in the introductory lecture outlines was that if enough people in the world were to practice TM®, there would be no more wars and we would experience world peace for the first time. Otherwise the introductory lectures were rather dry. They appealed to the idealism in most people and promised essentially four areas of benefits:

1. The use of one hundred percent of our mental potential.
2. Excellent physical health.
3. Naturally correct social behavior.
4. World peace.

During one evening meeting someone asked Maharishi, "Why can't we tell people about all of this marvelous spiritual advice to interest them in TM®?" Maharishi's answer took the whole evening. His answer contained three main points:

1. This is a scientific age, not a religious age. So we must temporarily set aside the delicate expressions of spiritual regeneration and speak in the hard and practical terms of science.

2. We don't want people to choke on too much information before they have enough experience to be able to understand this advanced wisdom. So we only teach one percent of what we know.

3. Maharishi wished he had never called the technique Transcendental Meditation in the first place because he found it frightened many people. He said it would

have been more popular if it had been called "Brand X."

He was also concerned that there were many other Eastern techniques of meditation in the market place today and that, to avoid any possible public association between his teaching and these others, it would be best to avoid the esoteric topics altogether. He felt strongly that all other traditions of spiritual development available today are steeped in ignorance and misunderstandings of the ancient Vedic Hindu religious documents from which TM® stems.

It made sense; here we had a technique that certainly seemed to work. It was relaxing, it increased our energy level during the day, and it promised to take us to the highest possible attainment of human development without effort. Everyone would want that! So why create problems for all the potential meditators in the world by presenting controversial information to them before they got a taste of the down-to-earth benefits like relaxation? If the nature of the more advanced material might keep people from trying TM® in the first place, then it might be wiser to save it for later—until after they had learned the technique.

By this time I was so stuffed with Maharishi's glowing promises that I was swallowing everything he served up with the firm conviction that this was indeed the truth of life. The world outside the course was full of stress and suffering: why shouldn't TM® be the answer? It was so logical. If people are tired they get frustrated; that leads to an accumulation of stress that in turn leads to an inability to get along with other people. So if TM® releases stress through the deep rest it provides, we can follow the logic backward and come up with a world of fulfilled people working together in harmony. We were so lucky to be cushioned from the stressful world by this great teaching. There was a strong feeling among many of us that it would be nice to be able to stay in a course like this forever.

One night I had my initial personal meeting with Maharishi. One of the meditators had requested over the microphone at an evening meeting that Maharishi check his mantra for him. Maharishi told him to come up after the meeting and he would take care of it. Talk about copycats! Almost everyone in the hall had the same request—and I wasn't going to be left out.

After the meeting we all waited our turns and one at a time went up to Maharishi to have him confirm for us that, indeed, we had the correct pronunciation of our mantras. He did this by having us whisper our mantras to him; he would whisper them back to us if we needed any correcting or fine-tuning. He reminded us that it was not necessary to have a crystal-clear pronunciation of it during meditation, but it was important to *know* the correct pronunciation. What a powerful experience to be so close to an enlightened man! I felt special, and so did everyone else. There were several hundred people who had their mantras checked that evening. I was impressed to see that he was able to remember the correct pronunciation for what I assumed were so many different mantras.

On another special evening Maharishi performed the puja with the initiators singing along. Everyone floated out of the lecture hall that night with the vision of Maharishi bowing before the altar of Guru Dev.

That one-month course left me well-primed to take the next step up the ladder to becoming a TM® teacher. I felt like an extremely special individual—now privy to the well-kept secrets of the universe. Many new words had been added to my vocabulary. I was certain I was speeding down that evolutionary highway to Cosmic Consciousness.

Learning the Enlightenment Business

After working for three months as a gravedigger at the Grove Street Cemetery in New Haven, I borrowed $865 from my parents and was on my way to Estes Park, Colorado in early October of 1970. The TM® movement had taken over the YMCA camp in Estes Park and was offering a two-and-half month teacher training course to complete the training begun during the one month course which had taken place that summer. (Immediately following the Poland Spring course, Maharishi had flown to Humboldt State College in Arcata, California, where he held a duplicate course.)

At Estes Park we would become "exponents of reality," according to Maharishi. We were already "knowers of reality," and now we would learn how to teach other people the way to transcend the relative world of ignorance and suffering. In order to accomplish this, there were two more steps to take. First, we had to learn the puja; that would involve a couple of months. Second, we had to learn the mantras—and how to select the right mantra for the right person.

So we had our work cut out for us. In addition to these two items, we would also learn how to present a second preparatory lecture, which mainly involved explaining how the mantra works and how to run the three days of follow-up instruction after initiation.

Throughout the entire course we were all involved in a heavy program of rounding. In the middle of the course, we were rounding 24 hours a day for a period of almost a week.

I have already described briefly the rounding we did at the Poland Spring course. At Estes Park, however, the rounding began as soon as we woke up. This meant that in the morning when we awoke we would sit up in our beds, close our eyes and begin thinking our mantra. If we fell back asleep, upon awakening we would sit up in bed and again begin thinking our mantra. If we still felt sleepy and dozed off, we would simply lie back down and go to sleep. This would continue until a full meditation was completed. For different people that might have been anywhere from twenty minutes to an hour. Then we would get out of bed, freshen up and do our asanas. There were ten of them, which took a little more than five minutes, at the end of which we would begin doing the breathing exercises. This was designed to relax us even further.

After five minutes of the pranayama, we would begin thinking our mantra with our eyes closed and continue with another full meditation. Another five-minute period of pranayama followed the end of the meditation. That was rounding. Assuming that a person slept for eight hours a night, he or she would spend a minimum of 14 hours a day in his room and by the middle of the course as much as 24 hours either rounding or sleeping. We had little or no contact with radio or television, no stereos, no movies and no entertainment in the traditional sense. At one point during the course a couple of pundits (Vedic scholars) were flown in from India, and for a couple of evenings we listened to them chant from the Vedas. The meaning of their chants was not explained, but it was supposed to produce a very spiritual atmosphere that would be conducive to our "evolution."

Many people in the course didn't sleep during the entire week of long rounding. Many of us ate very infrequently and relied on the sustenance we derived from a drink which we would make in our rooms from the juice of one lime, a teaspoon of honey and a cup of hot water. Rumor had it that this was a special Maharishi drink. Many people went into "silence" and didn't speak for a few weeks after that. They would wear signs around their necks or badges pinned to their shirts indicating that they were observing silence. That way no one would disturb them and they could maintain a deep level of rest even when in the dining hall or at lectures. Low metabolism was the name of the game. The less activity performed, the more stress would be released and the sooner one would "hit" CC.

Logically, one would expect to hear reports of heavy unstressing as a result of this intense rounding and, sure enough, it was happening. Eric, who attended the course with me, had the experience of literally being thrown across the room and onto the floor from his quiet meditative pose on his bed. This was attributed to "unstressing" (now I view it differently—see Chapter 9). A young girl reported seeing a large pair of green eyes floating around her room, staring at her. She ran out of her room, terrified by the experience. Maharishi assured her it was nothing to worry about. "Just some unstressing," he would say. "This is all very good, nothing to be concerned about."

A few days later another course participant saw the same set of green eyes floating around her room during meditation and claimed that even with her eyes opened she still saw them. "More unstressing," we were assured.

A number of people began experiencing involuntary bodily movements, twitchings and assorted repetitive and rhythmic involuntary movements of the head. What was going on? Just some very good heavy unstressing. We were advised to do lots of asanas (the yoga postures) and lots of pranayama (the breathing exercise) and "Take it as it comes." Truthfully, we all thought these experiences were kind of "neat" and, in a rather bizarre sense, even status symbols of sorts, although Maharishi discouraged placing any great emphasis on them. He always instructed us to keep our sights on the great goal of bringing the absolute into the relative, of building the state of eternal freedom of CC into our awareness.

We attended lectures by Maharishi every evening; during the day we rounded and had small group meetings where we practiced the checking procedure, lecturing, and initiation procedure with mock mantras such as "flower" and "carnation."

The meals were good and plentiful. Maharishi discouraged eating meat, but there were plenty of vegetables and dairy products and usually either fish or poultry. I had been a vegetarian since 1969 and so was delighted with the menu.

About three weeks into the course, during a solemn evening in the meeting hall, we received our individual copies of *The Holy Tradition* from Maharishi. This was the book which contained the puja ceremony with its translation, underlying meanings and its history (I have reprinted it here as Appendix 2). It was an evening we had all been eagerly awaiting. As Maharishi personally handed us our copies of the book, we each bowed our heads reverently before him. From then on we began learning and practicing the puja every day until the end of the course. Chapter 4 covers this experience in detail.

So the design of the course built us up to feel that we were very special people who had the answer to everybody's problems. And when we left the course, it was our obligation to go out and spread this knowledge to the poor people in stress city so humanity might be freed from ignorance and suffering.

The last few weeks of the course finally came, and it was time for us to get our mantras. We would use these to teach other people how to meditate. The mantras were the final key. We had already gained the deep experience of long meditation which rid us of a great deal of stress. We had learned the puja ceremony, which would be used to create the proper circumstances to give the potential meditator his mantra; and of course we had gained a tremendous body of knowledge about the truth of life. The mantras were the final ingredient to make us true "exponents of reality."

There was tight security surrounding the mantra instruction. Maharishi was in a special room in the hotel on the grounds. A schedule was posted with everybody's name on it indicating when, during the next four or five days, the individual would meet with Maharishi to receive his mantras. Except for the time we were individually scheduled to be there, we couldn't get near the immediate vicinity.

When my appointment time came, I headed for the hotel. There were large tables set out upon which sat hundreds of puja sets. These were the brass trays, candle holders, incense holders, camphor holders and small dishes. All of these same implements had been at my initiation ceremony in 1968.

We had all been briefed on the details of this ultimate initiation ceremony. We were joining the Holy Tradition. The making of the initiators was handled in pairs. As we entered Maharishi's room, there were three puja tables in a row. My partner and I stood on each side of Maharishi at the puja tables. We each had our own altar.

We performed the puja aloud with Maharishi, so he

could hear us and judge how well we were able to perform it. He was also checking our pronunciation and memorization of the Sanskrit.

When we finished the puja with him, we knelt down together before the pictures of Guru Dev. Then Maharishi sent me across the room to sit in a chair while he gave my partner his mantras. I could overhear the whispers but I really couldn't clearly discern anything.

My partner left. Maharishi asked me to come over, and then I received my mantras. In Chapter 3 I list the mantras and discuss the method I was given for assigning them to the new meditators.

This was about a week before the course ended. During those final days everyone took his turn receiving a set of mantras. Finally, a few days before the end of the course, we all had completed that final step. Now we were all initiators. What excitement!

In the midst of all this excitement a meeting was held during which we were all required to sign a pledge of loyalty. It was written in quasi-legal, devotionally spiritual terminology, and I have reprinted it here as Appendix 1. It amounted essentially to an oath of silence which we promised to maintain about the esoteric secrets of the principles and practice of TM®. I recall that it put a kind of damper on the festivities. We all wondered why it should be necessary to sign an official pledge of this sort. Maharishi offered the explanation that it was just in case some day an initiator began to "unstress too heavily" and made the movement his "object of unstressing." This would protect the teaching, he said. Chapter 10 explains why I can no longer keep silent about the dishonesty being perpetrated by the movement against people both in and out of it.

During one of Maharishi's final "pep talks" he remarked how exciting this course had been for all the angels who were in attendance. He said it had been as valuable an experience for the angels as it had been for us. Apparently a large group of angels had been in attendance through the entire two and a half months!

He explained further that the angels were jealous of human beings because we were able to meditate; they didn't have the ability to practice TM®. He said life was so glorious in their celestial realm that they found it difficult even to close their eyes, let alone to meditate. Because of this they couldn't experience the fulfillment of the peace and silence of the Absolute. We'll be considering this in later chapters.

The entire course generated a devotional attitude toward Maharishi, Guru Dev and all of the yogis and deities listed in the Holy Tradition.

I had now learned how to check a person's meditation, how to teach a three-day course in the practice of TM®, how to give introductory and follow-up preparatory lectures, how to perform the puja, and how to impart mantras. These were the qualifications of an "exponent of reality."

In addition, we had witnessed the birth of a new packaging concept for Maharishi's teachings. He called it the Science of Creative Intelligence. It was a new way of explaining all the TM® material in less esoteric terms. For the most part, he drew upon secular and scientific terminology. He had experimented with the idea at a few evening lectures and apparently was satisfied with the results. Today the entire movement revolves around the SCI conceptual framework.

On the last day of the course many people had final questions of a personal nature for Maharishi. We all gathered at Maharishi's quarters. In four hours or so Maharishi's plane would be departing from Denver, almost an hour's drive from Estes Park, so Maharishi didn't have much time to spare. We waited our turns to see him privately in his bedroom.

The questions ranged from mundane ones about college plans, work plans, etc. to those of a more "spiritual nature." Some of us were eligible to receive advanced techniques and wanted to receive them from Maharishi himself (although others in the movement were also qualified to impart them). Advanced techniques are additional practices, such as expansion of one's current mantra, which supposedly speed up spiritual advancement.

I was there to get two additional mantras to initiate my parents while visiting them on my way back to New Haven. I also wanted to get my second technique. I had been meditating two and a half years and was therefore eligible for it. At that time it was known as a "night technique." I received it that afternoon from Maharishi.

The instruction was very simple: when I went into his room, I knelt on the floor beside his bed; he told me that at night, as I was going to bed, I should prop a couple of pillows under my head, focus my attention at a position directly beyond my nose, and treat that focus of my attention as I would my mantra. In other words, if I found that my attention wandered, I should not try to force it back until I realized that my awareness was elsewhere. He said, "Now, just use this every night before you go to sleep." I received no explanation of what it was supposed to do, although I assumed it was going to speed up my progress toward cosmic consciousness.

After receiving my second technique, I asked Maharishi if I could receive some additional mantras. These would be for my parents. I was going to be visiting them shortly and I wanted to teach them how to meditate. I didn't know whether they would be open to it, but I wanted to be prepared.

He gave me the additional mantras and we exchanged the traditional salutation "Jai Guru Dev," meaning "Praise to Guru Dev." I stood up and left the room, returned to my quarters and packed my gear in order to be ready to leave immediately after seeing Maharishi off.

Everyone from the course was waiting outside as Maharishi headed to the shiny new rented Chrysler. The driver was Charlie Lutes, who was then (and is still) the director of the Spiritual Regeneration Movement, another of the five main branches of the TM® movement. Maharishi received flowers from many of the initiators and was fully loaded down with them by the time he reached the car. As soon as he was seated and the door was closed, Jerry Jarvis leaned down and exchanged a few words with Maharishi. A moment later the shiny new Chrysler left a cloud of dust behind as it sped down the dirt road to the camp exit. Maharishi stuck the armload of flowers out the window and began waving them up and down as the wind blew them out of his hands.

That was my last memory of Estes Park high in the Colorado Rockies: the sight of the Chrysler speeding out of camp with many new teachers scrambling in the dust to pick up the wind-blown flowers and petals dropped by Maharishi. We were now true executives in the consciousness industry working for the number one company in the field, Maharishi's Enlightenment, Inc.

Chapter Three

SUPERHYPE:
HOW MANTRAS ARE CHOSEN

I was twenty years old at the time I became a teacher of TM®—hardly an age to command respect, to emanate authority and to appear a fount of wisdom. Maharishi is quite shrewd and well understood that someone beyond thirty might feel uncomfortable being instructed by someone as young as I was. So he put a simple rule into effect which divided us on the basis of age into two categories—those who became initiators of students and people under thirty, and those who dealt with people over thirty.

The following shows the method for choosing the mantras as it was given to me personally by Maharishi on December 20, 1970, in Estes Park, Colorado. Note that the list ends at age thirty.

Age in Years	Male	Female
5-10	*Ing* (walking technique)*	*Im* (walking technique)
10-16	*Ing*	*Im*
16-30	*Aaing*	*Aaim*

*The walking technique, also known as the children's technique, is a quiet vocalization of the mantra. It is used by children when they are playing or on their way to school. The children's technique is taught in the same manner as the adult meditation except the repetition is never taken to the mental level. Its purpose is to dispel unhappiness.

That's all there was to it! No great mystical wisdom. No in-depth study of the esoteric "science of sound." No high-level interpretation of personality types in order to be able to assign these "highly personalized" sounds. Maharishi was able to instruct me in the secret of selecting mantras *in less than two minutes.* There were no other times during the entire course when this particular information was the subject of discussion or course work. And we were told in no uncertain terms that we should never discuss the mantras with anyone—not even among ourselves as initiators. Clearly, the movement was founded on an unquestioning faith in the honesty, integrity and trustworthiness of the leader, Maharishi.

My awe for the initiators was now somewhat diluted with the realization that there was apparently nothing very special about the mantras. I had received four of them, one of which was already my own, and I had been using it for two and a half years at that point. The "special air" around the initiators, I thought, must be that they all knew there was no tremendously complex or transcendental knowledge behind Maharishi's trade secret. It seemed the important thing was to maintain the air of mystery. That was the magnetic force at work. That was the real trade secret. It took more than $1,300 and almost four months of esoteric training to have this simple piece of information revealed to me.

After an investment of that magnitude, a careful and thoughtful analysis of the situation should have been in order. However, my youthful idealism and urge to hero worship were deeply ingrained. My "let-down feeling" didn't last long—in a very short time I was raring to go out and bestow knowledge of "reality" on the ignorant, suffering world.

There were some very good "party line" reasons why it was important to maintain complete secrecy about the way mantras are chosen. It went something like this: we, the initiators, believed we were very special people. There was even a widely-held view that all of the people in Maharishi's movement were reincarnations of already highly-evolved souls. These souls had been waiting on the "other side," in some cases for centuries, until just the right time to incarnate for their last trip through this human physical realm. The belief engendered by Maharishi's teaching was that once an individual attained the state of cosmic consciousness, he would never again be reincarnated as a lowly human with a gross physical body (as opposed to a "subtle" body). When a person in CC "drops his body," according to Maharishi, he simply moves into a subtler body and continues evolving and growing in even more majestic ways. Supposedly, as part of the great cosmic plan (which was perpetually unfolding itself), Maharishi and his master Guru Dev had come as one of the many intermittent revivals of the ancient wisdom of the "truth of life." We (as souls on the other side) had decided to put our "incarnate" orders through sometime back in the 40's and 50's. In this way, by the time we reached adulthood, we would be able to put in some time with Maharishi here in the flesh. He, as the master, would then help us to quickly melt away the stress that was standing between us and the unbounded freedom of the first stage of enlightenment, CC.

As one of our duties on this path, we were obligated to bring the rudiments of evolutionary enlightened wisdom to the stressed-out ignorant people who so desperately needed our guidance. Therefore, since we were so much more advanced than any of our potential initiates, we were capable of grasping the significance of TM® in the "big picture," which is the perpetually unfolding cosmic plan which involves belief in reincarnation and a great deal of other Hindu esoterica. If it were common knowledge that the choosing of the mantras was such a simple procedure, people might feel that there would be no need to learn TM® from qualified instructors, namely us. This would be grossly unfair to the potential meditator since we *knew* we were holding the truth of life. We were enlightened and they were ignorant: it was as simple as that. There would be no other way for the poor innocents to gain enlightenment within less than twenty lifetimes. It was our job to make sure that there were no barriers to their learning TM® now. We *knew* it was for their own good. What harm could a few half-truths do, as long as they took the course?

Therefore, we were taught to give the impression in public lectures that months of training were involved in learning to choose mantras and that it would not do justice to the teaching or to the student if we were to "explain" in hurried fashion just how the mantras *were* selected. When asked about them, I used to say, "A little bit of knowledge can be dangerous." How true that was! If people knew how easy it was to get a mantra, they'd probably never pay for the course. That would be dangerous to the finances of the movement, let alone to their own evolution, and more importantly to our (the teachers') evolution. It was economic and spiritual greed, pure and simple! But you couldn't have told me that then.

Why not? As I mentioned in the previous chapter, we were all well-programmed to believe that any negative emotion or reaction was nothing more than the expression of some release of stress. So I rationalized my initial reaction to learning how to select mantras—a reaction that was simply shock at the bald dishonesty of it—as "just some unstressing." This, of course, provided movement leaders and Maharishi with a most convenient way to avoid dealing with legitimate complaints about almost anything, particularly any doubts we may have had about the TM® technique or the movement.

So we were taught to lead the public into believing that there was some great mystery about how mantras are chosen when in fact there was only a very simple formula which we followed mechanically:

1. Check the age of the initiate on the interview form.
2. Check the sex of the initiate on the interview form.
3. Take these two pieces of information, plug them into the grid and then extract the "proper" mantra.

In all fairness to the teachers of TM®, it was not really a

complete "hype" on their part. We told people that the mantras were chosen individually to conform to their particular requirements, and in truth this was what we did—it is still being done today. We *did not* say, however, that those requirements were simply their age and sex.

Another common explanation given by the movement about how, in general terms, the mantras are chosen is that each individual will find different qualities of sounds soothing to his or her personality or physical type. Therefore, the right selection of a mantra is of vital importance. I must have dished out hours of that and similar half-truths and double-talk in my four years as a teacher.

To argue that the system of choosing mantras does not really take into account significant individual differences would be unfair if the argument were based solely on the grid at the beginning of this chapter. But it isn't.

Superhype

In addition to the four mantras shown in the grid, Maharishi also gave me two more mantras with which I could initiate my parents if they were interested. I was told to use them only for my parents until such time as I became an initiator of adults. (That occurred the following summer in 1971 when I spent a month with Maharishi in Amherst, Massachusetts at a combination teacher training course for meditators and a rest-and-relaxation course for teachers.) The mantras I received for my parents were:

Father (age 51) — *Shyaama*

Mother (age 46) — *Shyaam*

As it turned out, my parents were cooperative and I made use of the two mantras only days after I had received them from Maharishi. I didn't use them again until after the "go-ahead" from Maharishi which I received in the summer of 1971. At that time he told me to use them for anyone above the age of 30, *Shyaama* for males and *Shyaam* for females. It had only been six months since I had first been made an initiator of students, but Maharishi felt that I had initiated enough in that six-month period to gain the experience required to deal appropriately with adults.

In the spring of 1973, my wife Susan (whom I met through the movement in 1972) attended the teacher training course offered by Maharishi in La Antilla, on the southern Atlantic coast of Spain, near Portugal. We'll be examining some of the events that took place at that course in later chapters. For now let's take a look at the set of mantras and the method of choosing them that she received directly from Maharishi at that course.

The setting was a huge tent set on the beach. Maharishi sat on a flower-decked dais at the front of the "hall." There were fifty desk and chair positions facing Maharishi. Each of the desks was outfitted with a set of headphones wired to Maharishi's microphone. In this way Maharishi could speak privately to each of the 50 would-be teachers simultaneously without being heard by any bystanders.

Here is the list of mantras and age categories given to my wife, along with 49 other meditators on that summer afternoon.

Age	Mantra
10-12	*Eng*
12-14	*Em*
14-16	*Enga*
16-18	*Ema*
18-20	*Aeng*
20-22	*Aem*
22-24	*Aenga*
24-26	*Aema*
26-30	*Shiring*
30-35	*Shirim*
35-40	*Hiring*
40-45	*Hirim*
45-50	*Kiring*
50-55	*Kirim*
55-60	*Shyam*
60-65 and older	*Shyama*

You can see that sometime between December 1970 and May 1973, Maharishi eliminated the use of the initiate's sex as a significant criterion for assigning mantras. It's also interesting to note that Maharishi spelled the mantras for the new initiators in this course. He did not do so for those of us who became teachers at Estes Park back in 1970. It seems reasonable to assume that *Ing* (males 5-16) and *Im* (females 5-16) from the grid are the same mantras as *Eng* (anyone 10-12) and *Em* (anyone age 12-14) above. The same would apply to *Aaing* (males 16-30) and *Aeng* (anyone 18-20), to *Aaim* (females 16-30) and *Aem* (anyone 20-22), to *Shyaam* (females over 30) and *Shyam* (anyone 55-60), and to *Shyaama* (males over 30) and *Shyama* (anyone over 60).

Maharishi had explained at Estes Park that he didn't want to give the spelling of the mantras because it was the sound that was important, not any particular set of letters. Perhaps he changed his mind as more and more people became initiators. He probably decided that the easiest way to avoid confusion on the pronunciation would be to give a spelling that would most clearly approximate the desired sound.

In view of this, the conclusion is a revelation of dishonesty. Let's look at the mantras which are common to both lists and see if the process of assigning them is consistent. That is, do we find a pattern of assigning them that is fixed or only random?

Mantra	As assigned (1970)	As assigned (1973)
Ing (Eng)	Male, 5-16	Anyone, 10-12
Im (Em)	Female, 5-16	Anyone, 12-14
Aaing (Aeng)	Male, 16-30	Anyone, 18-20
Aaim (Aem)	Female, 16-30	Anyone, 20-22
Shyaam (Shyam)	Female, 16-30	Anyone, 55-60
Shyaama (Shyama)	Male, over 30	Anyone, over 60

I don't know how many other variations in the methods of choosing mantras Maharishi may have employed at other teacher training courses, but I do know of at least one additional mantra that was used by Maharishi as part of the TM® technique. That mantra is *Ram,* which John White points out in *Everything You Want to Know about TM (Pocket Books, 1976) is "one of the Hindu names of God."*

Although other mantras may be unknown to me, we can see clearly enough from these two methods that whichever one is used to assign a particular mantra to a person, it is not as crucially significant as the TM® movement would like the public to believe. For example, I am now 26 years old. If I were to learn TM® from a teacher who had been trained during the course my wife attended and had received his mantras in the same group as my wife, then I would be given the mantra *Shiring.* I would be led to believe that this was chosen for me according to an ancient foolproof system of selecting mantras which came down to us through the grace of Maharishi's guru and then Maharishi himself. If, on the other hand, I were to learn TM® from a teacher trained during the course I attended, we can assume (although we can't be certain because other teachers may have received equally divergent methods of assigning mantras) that I would receive *Aeng (Aaing).*

It becomes obvious why Maharishi ordered us never to discuss mantras among ourselves. It would lead to confusion, he cautioned. How right he was! It leads directly to confusion—as well as to doubts about his motives and integrity. I expect many people in the TM® movement will feel there is nothing wrong with this deception—that whatever the reason, it must be right because Maharishi can do no wrong. The initiator's yardstick of right and wrong is Maharishi himself. If Maharishi does it or says it, then it is the truth—and no questions are asked, no matter how self-contradictory it may be.

An example of how people within the movement have been used as innocent, unknowing messengers of misrepresentation can be seen in this excerpt from the recent bestseller *TM** by Harold Bloomfield, Michael Cain and Dennis Jaffe (Dell edition, p. 44):

Because the TM® permits the meditator to experience quiet levels of the mind, where the influence of each thought is especially profound, the selection of the correct mantra for each individual is of critical importance. Maharishi and the thousands of trained teachers of the TM® technique rely on an ancient tradition through which many generations have fathomed the full depth of the mind. This tradition provides a systematic procedure for selecting the most suitable sounds for use in the technique of TM® by particular individuals. Such procedure has been maintained since 5000 B.C. or earlier, the time of mankind's most ancient teachings, the Vedas.

If this procedure of choosing mantras is so systematic and has been so carefully maintained for at least 6,970 years (according to Bloomfield, Cain and Jaffe), the logical question arises, Why in the next three years did the method change so radically? Why was the sexual difference between men and women no longer taken into account when choosing the mantra for a person? It would seem that the ancient tradition Maharishi was drawing upon is properly called "pulling the wool over everyone's eyes."

Several more instructive examples of meditator gullibility can be seen in Patricia Drake Hemingway's *The Transcendental Meditation Primer* (Dell, 1976). In her attempt to write an honest and supportive document about TM®, Ms. Hemingway became a victim of the same deception. Through the misinformation she received from her TM® instructors and informants, she unintentionally authored certain misinformation about the mantras and the process by which they are selected. On page 11 of the abridged (Dell Purse Book) edition we find, *"Scholars of meditation say that each individual differs in the quality of the sounds that are most soothing to his individual personality and physical type. The right selection of a mantra is of vital importance."* As we have already seen, the personality has absolutely nothing to do with the selection of a mantra. The physical type did have a part in the selection process as of 1970, but not in 1973. The ancient tradition seems to have been seriously tampered with—or else never existed as such.

Again on page 13 we find Ms. Hemingway stating, *"Our teachers spend much time and study to be able to assign the proper mantra to the right person. It is not random."* And on page 22 is more obvious misinformation: *"There are different mantras given to different people. For example, heads of industry get different mantras than housewives and mystics."* No mention was made in either of the mantra selection processes described in this chapter that one iota of consideration was given to an individual's occupation or position in life when choosing his mantra.

The truly sad part about this particular aspect of the TM® deception is not the hype wherein the TM® teacher deceives the new initiate. Rather, it is the superhype wherein Maharishi himself deceives his followers. The thousands of TM® teachers who have made him and his movement so popular have been used as pawns to spread lies for the advancement of Maharishi's own ends. The hype itself was not so blatantly dishonest. But to be dishonest to those who love you and hold you in high regard is truly a superhype— one which demands serious attention by all those who feel concern for the truth. Maharishi talks in glittering terms about the "truth of life." Why, then, does he employ deceptive techniques to bring people into his movement and to con those who are already in the movement into carrying his lies abroad? If deception resides at the basis of the TM® technique, then it behooves us to look at some of the other claims made by the TM® movement.

Chapter Four

WORSHIPPING FALSE GODS: THE PUJA CEREMONY AND THE HOLY TRADITION

By the time I received my copy of *The Holy Tradition* from Maharishi that October evening at the YMCA Camp in Estes Park, Colorado, I had witnessed the performance of the puja ceremony perhaps five times. The first was when I was initiated. On that occasion any importance attributed to it had been intentionally downplayed by my teacher. "I will perform a brief ceremony which you will only observe," she said. What a contrast to the statement by Jerry Jarvis at the Estes Park course! "Initiation (imparting of the mantra) without the puja is like a Cadillac without gas." In other words, TM® won't work without the puja.

So apparently my initiator, Marilyn, for reasons which will become clear in this chapter, was attempting to place the least amount of importance on the ceremony. Keeping everyone off guard with a sweet facade of sincerity was another game we learned as we became initiators.

The next few times I saw the puja performed was at Poland Spring, with Maharishi at the altar. Each of these occasions was treated as if we were incredibly fortunate to have this opportunity because "this is real inner circle stuff." The same was true at Estes Park the few times Maharishi performed the puja prior to our receiving *The Holy Tradition* booklets. We all treated those occasions as expressions of a sort of spiritual intercourse between Maharishi and us.

A pungent aroma of idol-worship was definitely present. We had little idea what the puja really meant, and yet we all bowed down with Maharishi when he completed his offerings after each performance of it. We were obviously relying on Maharishi more than reasonableness would ordinarily permit.

As we received our orange-covered paperbound copies of *The Holy Tradition,* we returned to our seats in the hall. Interestingly, the hall was the camp church. Upon opening to the first page we found printed at the top of the page:

JAI GURU DEV
Introduction to the Holy Tradition

After two and a half years of being programmed to revere the initiators and their secret wisdom, I felt as if I were holding TOP SECRET HIGHLY CLASSIFIED CONFIDENTIAL papers in my hands.

That night Jerry Jarvis read aloud to us, word for word, the entire text from cover to cover. The English translation of the "Invocation to the Holy Tradition" follows here, but I have reprinted the entire text of the booklet in Appendix 2. Bear in mind that this is what the movement publicly declares is merely an innocuous way of saying "Thank you."

INVOCATION OF THE HOLY TRADITIONS
Whether pure or impure, or whether full of purities or
    impurities,
Whosoever remembers the lotus-eyed Lord gains inner
    and outer purity.

INVOCATION

To Lord Narayan, to lotus-born Brahma the Creator,
to Vaishistha, to Shakti and his son Parashar,
To Vyasa, to Shukadeva, to the great Gaudapada, to
Govinda, ruler among the yogis, to his disciple
Shri Shankaracharya, to his disciples Padma-Padam,
Hasta-Malakam,
To him, Trotakacharya, to Vartik-kar, to others, to the
Tradition of our Masters, I bow down.

To the abode of the wisdom of the Shrutis, Smritis and
Puranas, to the abode of kindness, to the feet of the
Lord Shankaracharya, to the emancipator of the
world, I bow down.
To Shankaracharya the emancipator, hailed as Krishna
and Badarayana, to the commentator of the Brahma
Sutras, I bow down. to the Lord I bow down again
and again.

At whose door the whole galaxy of gods pray for
perfection day and night.
Adorned by immeasurable glory, preceptor of the whole
world, having bowed down to Him, we gain
fulfillment.
Skilled in dispelling the cloud of ignorance of the
people, the gentle emancipator, Brahmananda
Saraswati, the supreme teacher, full of brilliance,
on Him we meditate.

Offering invocation to the lotus feet of Shri Guru Dev, I
bow down.
Offering a seat to the lotus feet of Shri Guru Dev,
I bow down.
Offering a bath to the lotus feet of Shri Guru Dev,
I bow down.
Offering a cloth to the lotus feet of Shri Guru Dev,
I bow down.

Offering sandal paste to the lotus feet of Shri Guru Dev,
I bow down.
Offering full unbroken rice to the lotus feet of Shri
Guru Dev, I bow down.
Offering a flower to the lotus feet of Shri Guru Dev,
I bow down.
Offering incense to the lotus feet of Shri Guru Dev,
I bow down.
Offering light to the lotus feet of Shri Guru Dev,
I bow down.
Offering water to the lotus feet of Shri Guru Dev,
I bow down.
Offering fruit to the lotus feet of Shri Guru Dev,
I bow down.
Offering water to the lotus feet of Shri Guru Dev,
I bow down.
Offering betel leaf to the lotus feet of Shri Guru Dev,
I bow down.
Offering coconut to the lotus feet of Shri Guru Dev,
I bow down.

Offering camphor flame

White as camphor, the incarnation of kindness, the
essence of creation garlanded by the Serpent King,
Ever dwelling in the lotus of my heart, Lord Shiva
with Mother Divine, to Him I bow down.

Offering light to the lotus feet of Shri Guru Dev,
I bow down.
Offering water to the lotus feet of Shri Guru Dev,
I bow down.

Offering a handful of flowers to the lotus feet of
Shri Guru Dev, I bow down.

Guru is the glory of Brahma, Guru is the glory of
Vishnu, Guru is the glory of the great Lord Shiva,

Guru is the supreme Transcendent personified;
therefore to Shri Guru Dev, adorned by glory,
I bow down.

The Unbounded as the endless canopy of the sky, the
Omnipresent in all creation, the sign of That has
been revealed by Him who was That; there to Him,
to Shri Guru Dev, I bow down.

Guru Dev, Shri Brahmananda, in the glory of the bliss
of the Absolute, in the glory of transcendental joy,
in the glory of Unity, the very embodiment of
knowledge, who is beyond the universe like the sky,
as the goal of "That thou art" and other (Shrutis
which grant eternal Unity of life),

The One, the Eternal, the Pure, the Immovable, the
Witness of all intellects, whose status transcends
thought, the Transcendent along with the three
gunas, the true preceptor, to Shri Guru Dev,
I bow down.
The blinding darkness of ignorance has been removed
by the application of the ointment of knowledge, the
eye of knowledge has been opened by Him; therefore
to Him, to Shri Guru Dev, I bow down.

Offering a handful of flowers to the lotus feet of
Shri Guru Dev, I bow down.

The method of learning the puja began, then, with a
number of meetings at which Maharishi slowly spoke the
Sanskrit to the whole group. We listened and then, word by
word, repeated the entire invocation along with him. The
same method is used by many foreign-language teachers.

We worked on the Sanskrit section for two or three days
with Maharishi, and when we had it pretty well learned, we
began working in small groups to perfect our memorization
of its exact and precise pronunciation.

59

The next step was to memorize the English translation, first word-for-word and then phrase-for-phrase. As you can see in the Appendix, the text was laid out for purposes of teaching in this manner. Having completed that, we began to memorize the underlying meanings of the expressions we had learned.

All of this rote learning required a great deal of time and concentration on our part as students, and it is perhaps one of the reasons we felt we could tell people in somewhat good conscience that it took a great deal of time to learn how to select mantras. Obviously, learning the puja had nothing to do with the mantra selection process. However, we couldn't impart mantras without first performing the puja. So, we figured, learning the puja and selecting mantras were one and the same. But at the time we were learning the puja, we actually knew no more about how to choose mantras than any other meditator off the street.

The statement on the first page of the orange booklet certainly made us curious.

>"The purpose of the Invocation is to tune our active mind, through the memory of the great masters, to the goal of their wisdom, the Absolute, and from there pick up the mantra and give it to the new initiate; and through that lead his consciousness to the Absolute."

What then did that mean about how we would choose the mantras? It strongly implies that we were going to become masters of a cosmic ability to cognize ancient secret sounds from out of some astral plane. Of course, we all knew the difference between the Absolute and astral planes. At least we believed we did; in any case, we had heard from Maharishi some intellectual-sounding discourses about the difference between the two.

The lure of joining an esoteric inner circle with a monopoly on truth was very powerful. It was easy to overlook many inconsistencies between what was being taught and the fruits of that teaching.

Having learned the Sanskrit, its English translation, and

the underlying significance of the invocation, we then went on to learn the "motions." These are the programmed movements used by the teacher to make the offerings in the middle of the ceremony, and at a few other points during the chanting of the invocation.

We practiced the entire puja in our rooms, with makeshift puja sets of paper cups and plates, whenever we had the time from then on until the end of the course.

The statement "I bow down" is made 26 times during the performance of the puja. The physical act of bowing down before the altar of Guru Dev is performed once. There are six references made to the title Lord; two references to lord Shiva (another member of the Hindu diety); and a reference to lord Vishnu, yet another member of the Hindu polytheistic superstructure. Lord Narayan is mentioned in the opening phrase of the invocation. According to the explanation offered in the text on page 9,

> "Lord Narayana, the embodiment of eternal and Absolute Being, is the first custodian and the eternal lighthouse of the wisdom of integrated life, from Him it came on to Brahma, the Creator Padma-bhawam who is born of the lotus rooted in Absolute Being."

Note here that Maharishi would have us believe in Brahma as the creator. There is a reference to the "whole galaxy of gods praying for perfection day and night" at the door of Shankara. We also find that at the end of the puja, the last namah or "bowing down" is directed specifically to the lotus feet of Maharishi's deceased teacher, Guru Dev. This depicts an all-out act of worhsip which is accompanied by the physical act of kneeling before the altar with the head bowed and the palms together.

Keeping all of these facts in mind, let's look at a definition of religion from *Readers Digest Encyclopedic Dictionary:*

> "The beliefs, attitudes, emotions, behavior, etc. constituting man's relationship with the powers and

principles of the universe, especially with a deity or deities; also any particular system of such beliefs, attitudes, etc."

It seems that the puja ceremony and the information offered in the "Introduction to the Holy Tradition" fit this definition of religion.

In rebuttal, the movement might point out that Maharishi has written, we assumed the booklet was his work although nowhere in the text is it attributed to him, on page 31 of *The Holy Tradition:*

"We have seen how the truth of integration of life is handed on from generation to generation in great clarity, in great completeness, in great simplicity and in a natural way, through this Holy Tradition of Masters. It is this that forms the main trunk of the tree of knowledge from which different religions take their life to guide man from time to time, from generation to generation."

In other words, Maharishi is making the claim that the Holy Tradition—all the beliefs, attitudes, emotions and behavior intrinsic to it—is not a religion in and of itself but rather is *the source* of all religions, and hence could not conflict with *any* religions.

In the absence of any proof that this tradition is indeed the source of all religions, it becomes a matter of individual belief as to whether it is or not. As such, the entire body of Maharishi's teaching falls back onto the pile along with all the other religions from which Maharishi had attempted to divorce himself and his teachings.

Those of us who were "knowers of reality," however, *believed* that this tradition formed the basis of all religions. As a result, it was not difficult to make the following statements about the puja when questioned by interested potential meditators:

"It's just a secular offering of thanks."

"It's just a traditional Indian way of offering gratitude" (implying only a cultural difference).

"It's sort of like a party to celebrate the new meditator's learning of this ancient technique."

"Oh, no, it's definitely not religious."

"No, it won't conflict with your religion."
The last is given without even asking what the person's beliefs are!

And just in case the potential initiate still had some doubts about whether the ceremony was religious or not, I used to say, "The student is only asked to witness it. It is performed by the initiator and for the initiator to set the right circumstances for instruction." In this way, I used to tell myself, even if it turned out to be religious, there should be no need for the student to worry about any involvement with it.

And yet here again we find another problem. If the student is not a participant, why is he required to bring the fruit, flowers and handkerchief to be offered on the altar during the ceremony? And, also, why is he so strongly urged to join the initiator in the devotional act of bowing down at the end of the puja? And why, according to Maharishi and Jerry Jarvis, won't TM® work without the puja?

Is there a religion in the world with which these acts of worship conflict? Indeed there is. Well, then, what does that religion have to say about the TM® teaching?

Maharishi himself has acknowledged the existence of this religion: namely, Christianity. He has even said that he loves it. At a press conference held on the campus of Maharishi International University in Fairfield, Iowa, and reported in the *Fairfield Ledger* on 3 October 1975, Maharishi stated, "I am a priest and I love Christianity and religion, but I don't want TM® to fail."

It is a strong statement to say that you "love" anything. It implies a powerful element of appreciation and respect. It also implies a certain amount of responsibility to the object of that love. Since Maharishi himself brought up the topic of Christianity at the conference and even professed love for it, I feel it appropriate to consider his claim that "TM® does not conflict with any religion" in light of the Christian Bible.

There may well be other religions with which TM® is in conflict, but to keep things simple for purposes of examining Maharishi's claim that TM® is not in conflict with any religions, I will confine myself to a discussion centered upon Christian beliefs and attitudes.

Being a Christian means following the teachings and actions of Jesus Christ. What, then, did Jesus teach and believe? Let's take a look at some well-accepted quotes from the Bible. The scriptures used are from the *Revised Standard Version.*

In John 17:3 we find Jesus speaking in prayer to his Father in heaven:

> *And this is eternal life, that they know thee the only true God, and Jesus Christ Whom thou has sent.*

Jesus states in no uncertain terms that His heavenly Father is the only true God and also that to gain eternal life we must know God. In order to know God we must know His purpose for us, His commandments, His wishes, His personality, His qualities and His teachings. Also the statement is made that we must know His Son, Jesus. That would imply an understanding of Jesus and His role in the working out of God's purposes.

In John 20:17 Jesus is speaking to Mary Magdalene after He had risen from the tomb. He told her to go and tell His brothers that He was ascending to His Father in heaven.

> *Jesus said to her, "Do not hold me, for I have not yet ascended to the Father; but go to my brethren and say to them, 'I am ascending to my Father and your Father, to my God and your God!'"*

Jesus makes it clear here that the God He is referring to is not only His God but also the God of all true Christian believers. This means that according to Christ's teachings there is only one true God.

I Timothy 2:5 states,

> *For there is one God, and there is one mediator between God and men, the man Christ Jesus.*

This is a very interesting statement. Only one mediator between man and God—not two or three. Just one, and it is not Guru Dev, who is named as the mediator. That "one" is clearly identified as Jesus Christ Himself.

If the "Holy Tradition" is truly of divine origin, then it must acknowledge Jesus Christ as coming in the flesh. We find this stated in I John 4:1-3:

> Beloved, do not believe every spirit, but test the spirits to see whether they are of God; for many false prophets have gone out into the world. By this you know the Spirit of God: every spirit which confesses that Jesus Christ has come in the flesh is of God, and every spirit which does not confess Jesus is not of God.

Since the puja does not acknowledge Jesus, then it can't be in accord with Christian teachings.

The gods of the puja are clearly not the God whom Jesus made known. As we see in Exodus 3:15,

> God also said to Moses, "Say this to the people of Israel, the Lord, the God of your father, the God of Abraham, the God of Isaac, and the God of Jacob, has sent me to you: This is my name forever, and thus I am to be remembered throughout all generations."

The name referred to is found in the footnote at the bottom of the page in Exodus. It states that in the original Hebrew the divine name of the one true God is YHWH, commonly translated as Yahweh or Jehovah. God said that this was to be His name forever. This name does not appear in the puja in any form.

Then we find in I Corinthians 8:4-6,

> . . . we know that an idol has no real existence and that "there is no God but one." For although there may be so-called gods in heaven or on earth—as indeed there are many "gods" and many "lords"—yet for us there is one God, the Father, from whom are all things and for whom we exist, and one Lord, Jesus Christ, through whom are all things and through whom we exist.

Christian teaching recognizes the existence of other so-called "gods" and "lords." But there is really only one God, the Father and Creator, and one Lord, Jesus Christ, through whom the creation took place. So apparently worship can be directed either toward the one true God or toward these other "gods." Therefore these many gods of the puja, worshipped by the TM® movement, are, in Christian terms, false gods. The puja, as a form of worship, must by Christian definition be termed worship of false gods.

The proper way to worship the true Christian God is made crystal clear by Jesus Christ himself in John 4:23-24:

> *But the hour is coming, and now is when the true worshippers will worship the Father in spirit and truth, for such the Father seeks to worship Him. God is spirit, and those who worship Him must worship in spirit and truth.*

So there it is! True worship for a Christian is to be done in spirit and truth, not with images, photographs, paintings, deceit or dishonesty.

Christians cannot participate in false worship and still be true to their religion. This is in agreement with Paul's first letter to the Corinthian congregation. In 10:14 of that epistle he says, "Therefore, my beloved, shun the worship of idols."

The offerings of the fruit, flowers, and the handkerchief in the puja come from the initiate, so in being initiated into TM® he would be indirectly making offerings to false gods. And if he were to bow down with the initiator, having been deliberately deceived into thinking that the ceremony was purely secular, then he would be violating the commandment of God given in Exodus 20:4-5:

> *You shall not make yourself a graven image, or any likeness of anything that is in heaven above, or that is in the earth beneath, or that is in the water under the earth; you shall not bow down to them or serve them.*

Even an angel of God refused to accept a human's act of worship. As recorded in Revelation 22:8-9, we learn,

> *I John am he who heard and saw these things. And when I heard and saw them, I fell down to worship at*

the feet of the angel who showed them to me; but he said to me, "You must not do that! I am a fellow servant with you and your brethren the prophets, and with those who keep the words of this book. Worship God."

Here we see that any act of bowing down is not in keeping with God's commandments unless the bowing down is directed towards Yahweh or Jehovah. The Bible teaches us that a heavenly creature considers himself to be a fellow servant along with all human Christians, and therefore is himself unworthy to receive such devotional attention.

There is a closely guarded film owned by the TM® movement of the days when Maharishi was with Guru Dev. The film is no more than ten minutes in length. I have viewed it with Maharishi and a group of initiators on two or three occasions. It is referred to by the movement as the "Guru Dev Film." It contains a brief episode in which Guru Dev is seated on his throne in a bright orange silk robe receiving the worship of his followers. The puja ceremony, which I used to perform, was being performed directly to the man Guru Dev! This is certainly worship of a person, not worship of God. There is no biblical support anywhere for this form of worship.

The emphasis of Jesus's teachings was to live in accordance with the laws of God and His divine will as set down in the Bible. The TM® teaching, on the other hand, instructs us to contact the "Absolute" within us without making any effort even to live a righteous life, let alone seeking to gain God's favor. Moreover, the sources for the TM® teaching are clearly the Hindu tradition. So we find at the bottom line of this spiritual account sheet that TM® and Christianity are diametrically opposed.

Is this Maharishi's love for Christianity? Is this his respect for it? The TM® movement shows no sense of responsibility to the beliefs of Christianity. How, then, could Maharishi make the statement that he loves Christianity?

Maharishi's claim of love for Christianity seems to be as unfounded in truth as are the claims about the mantra selection process or the puja not being a religious act of worship.

If TM® is so good and beneficial, developing the highest qualities of humanity in people, must we conclude that honesty is not one of those qualities? Apparently Maharishi feels that this is the case. How can TM® be a "good thing" if the teachers of the technique are required not to tell the truth about it?

Can we trust the TM® movement's claim that the mantras are meaningless? I want to point out to those who feel that Christianity and TM® are compatible: you cannot serve two masters.

Chapter Five

WINNING THE WAR FOR MAHARISHI:
Research at the Institute of Living

In September, 1971, I began college as a freshman at the University of Connecticut. At that time the TM® movement was placing great emphasis on the value of medical and scientific research into the effects of TM®. A concerted effort was being made to coordinate all TM® research in progress around the world. In addition, a research index was published by the TM® movement which contained suggestions for areas of possible TM® research.

Achieving scientific credibility was a major goal of the TM® movement. In order to win the public relations war, the TM® movement decided that scientific support for their claims was required in order to remove TM® as far as possible from the esoteric and mystical realms from which mantras and meditation stem.

As a result many TM® teachers either began their own research projects or encouraged their contacts at research facilities and universities to initiate TM®-related research projects. I was familiar with the work of Drs. Robert Keith Wallace and Herbert Benson at the Harvard Medical School. They had been studying the physiological effects of TM® under clinical conditions, measuring heart rate, oxygen consumption, breathing rate, galvanic skin resistance, blood chemistry, and brain waves to see if the state of physical relaxation achieved during TM® was unique.

One of the major reasons I went to college was because Maharishi wanted his TM® instructors to have degrees. The truth of the matter was that I wanted CC more than a B.A. So I decided that while I was at school I would work on TM®-related projects. The result of this decision was that I designed a research project entitled "Comparative Physiological Effects of Transcendental Meditation and Deep Rest" and applied for an undergraduate research grant. I planned to purchase electrodes for measuring brain waves, along with assorted equipment needed for taking other physiological measurements. In addition, some of the funds would be used to compensate subjects drawn from the populace of the University of Connecticut campus for their time as subjects in the study. I was pleasantly surprised when my grant application for $400.00 was approved.

After many long, hard days and nights, a small laboratory was set up on the second floor of the Life Sciences Building. My research design called for measures of galvanic skin resistance, an indication of the ease with which a mild electrical current travels across the skin—say, the palm of an individual's hand. The theory behind this is that if anxiety, nervousness, or tension are present, a marked change will appear in the graphic record of the electrical impulse passing between the two electrodes. If relaxation continues for a period of time, the lines on the graph will show a dip that will remain constant throughout the period of relaxation. The same technique is used in lie detector tests.

I also measured breath rate, heart rate, and brain wave activity by means of a standard SONY tape recorder and an FM frequency converter which made it possible to record the brain waves on standard audio tape.

In order to analyze the brain wave tapes I would be collecting, I contacted Dr. Bernard Glueck, Director of Research at the Institute of Living in Hartford, since he was also involved in brain wave research and I knew he had an interest in TM® research. He was very helpful and cooperative. Also, his associate, Dr. Charles Stroebel, offered assistance with some of the technical matters.

After I recorded all the EEG data, Dr. Glueck offered to let me use one of his small lab computers to analyze the EEG tapes. However, the only time that I could use the computer was during the night when the laboratory was closed and the computer was not being used for other experiments.

One morning, near the end of my work at the Institute, Dr. Glueck offered me an opportunity to work on a major research project which would involve teaching the patients at the Institute of Living how to meditate and comparing the effects, both psychological and physiological, to the experiences of patients who would be instructed in a technique of biofeedback.

There were indications from other TM® research that alpha brain wave activity (7 to 13 cycles per second) increased in meditating subjects. Alpha waves are generally understood to be associated with a relaxed state of mind. The hope was that through biofeedback techniques a person could develop conscious control over the production of alpha waves and that this might in turn produce all of the other relaxation benefits and symptoms which TM® was believed to produce.

Needless to say, it sounded like an exciting opportunity, and I realized that I would probably be able to receive credit from the University of Connecticut while working on the project. As it turned out, this was the case, and I began working on the project in June, 1972.

Four teachers of TM® were on the research staff, including me. In addition, there were two other members of the team who had more traditional backgrounds. By this I simply mean that they were not TM®-oriented as we teachers were. We (the TM® teachers) were convinced that TM® was already a proven cure for almost everything, including the common cold; these tests were just formalities, the results of which were certain to be positive.

There were three groups of patients in the design of the experiment. One group learned TM®, one group learned the alpha biofeedback conditioning technique, and the third group learned other relaxation techniques from a staff psychologist.

Since many of the patients who were being instructed were anxious and nervous with a very short attention span, it was necessary to condense much of the TM® course material. Dr. Glueck emphasized the importance of not indoctrinating the patients with the philosophies of Maharishi (such as CC) or even extensive discussions on stress release. Rather, he said, pare the TM® experience down to its essentials. These were: the mantra, how to use it, and how to deal with any problems that might come up during the experience which would hinder the correct practice of the technique.

This posed certain problems for us as teachers of TM® because we felt the philosophy (what we called the "understanding of the experience") was a very important part of the technique. Eventually we all came around to appreciating the importance of this distinction between experience and philosophy being upheld under the circumstances at the Institute. We realized that if the results were positive in the patients practicing TM®, it would speak even more highly for the effectiveness of the technique because the understanding which Maharishi had emphasized as being so important would have been proven to be negligible for the success of the technique.

Dr. Glueck's attitude toward the project was seriously scientific. As a result, when a patient entered the program, we would sit down with him and have a very brief discussion, explaining that he would simply be learning TM®, a relaxation technique, and that it would be very easy. We said he would be learning a meaningless sound (the mantra), and that some physiological and psychological testing would be required. If he agreed to this, he would meet with one of the four TM® teachers, go through the initiation ceremony (the puja) and receive his mantra. A brief checking period on each of the following three days completed his instruction. Then he would come up to the research unit to meditate twice a day for the first few weeks. This would ensure that he did meditate and also that he had quiet surroundings in which to meditate.

My experience as a meditator and as a teacher of TM® provides me no alternative but to admit that relaxation does result from sitting down to practice TM® twice a day. I also strongly believe that rest and relaxation are healthy, beneficial and necessary for life to be truly enjoyable and satisfying. However, I also readily admit that TM® is not the only way to experience regular rest in order to maintain a healthy and active life.

TM® appeared to generate positive effects for many people in the study, and certain TM® subjects in the study responded quickly and positively to the practice of TM®. Other patients didn't enjoy it at all. I also remember one subject who refused to meditate shortly after learning how to do it. The explanation given for his refusal to meditate was this: TM® worked so well for him (meaning that it was causing rapid release of pent-up stress and tension) that he couldn't handle the rapid changes in his psychophysiological and emotional make-up. Therefore, he simply decided not to meditate at all.

In Appendix 5, "The Scientific Case Against TM®," John White considers these issues in greater depth. He brings out the very important fact that whatever may be the results of any research to date into the effects of TM®, they tell us nothing substantial because without the knowledge of what TM® really is and without adequate comparative research, any and all scientific claims about TM®'s uniqueness are simply unproven.

Eventually the project was dropped at the Institute. One of the major factors for its discontinuance was our intentional withholding of information, as required by the TM® movement. Even under strict research circumstances, we four teachers rigidly stuck to our oath of silence about the mantra selection process. We also stated that the mantras were meaningless. We did not admit to the religious nature of the puja. It now seems to me that in the interests of science and in the interests of really studying TM® honestly, this information should have been provided. The intentional concealment of information could only lead to unscientific research. For example, if the mantra selection process were known then, it might have been possible to test the different mantras against other known mantras to see if there were truly a measurable difference in the effects of each. In the absence of that information, all studies of TM® become nothing more than studies of a "black box."

As a result of these detailed investigations into the physiological effects of TM®, it did become obvious in certain cases that the mental repetition of the mantra had a powerful effect on the patterns of brain wave activity. I remember Dr. Glueck saying on occasion around the lab and in public, "If there's any magic to TM®, it's in the mantras." There were times when a subject was learning the technique while being monitored by the EEG equipment. At the moment during initiation when the mantra repetition became silent, there was a dramatic development of an unusual synchrony in the brain wave activity. In Chapters 8 and 9 I will consider one possible explanation of the magical effect of the mantras. In a nutshell, I suggest the possibility here that what is being measured is the subtle effect of a spirit realm on the mind of man.

Our deception at the Institute was a rather sad affair. We all knew that the puja had some religious significance, whether we admitted it to ourselves or not, and I assume we all knew that the mantras did have significant meanings. Obviously this information should have been made known—at least to Dr. Glueck—in fairness to him.

As it happened, however, not only was Dr. Glueck kept in the dark about TM®'s mysterious secrets, but in its usual zealous fashion the TM® movement latched onto the fact that research was beginning at the Institute of Living and began to spread the word that TM® was now an accepted cure for mental illness. As a result, part of our job as initiators on the project was to act as liaisons between Dr. Glueck and the movement in an effort to keep the public statements about the project in line with the truth that the project had just begun and that in fact there were absolutely no results to report.

I spent a total of six months working in the research department at the Institute of Living on the relaxation study and returned to my work at the university in January, 1973. My spiritual greed had been given some significant appeasement through the experience, but like most others in the enlightenment industry, the greed was still there, strong and hungry.

Chapter Six

SPIRITUAL GREED: TEACHING AS AN EXPRESSWAY TO ENLIGHTENMENT

In the last three chapters I have recorded my observations about the deception perpetrated by the TM® movement against the general public. In Chapter 3 I pointed out that the deception doesn't end there—it is even directed toward Maharishi's own followers—that through this deception they are manipulated to do Maharishi's will. I have posed the question several times, in one form or another, "Why is all this going on?"

There is an attitude—and it seems to be common within the movement—which I must now discuss at length in order to help you understand some of the reasons for these deceptions. This attitude can perhaps best be called "spiritual greed." To illustrate it, let's look at a few more examples of the kinds of deception I overlooked because I, too, felt this particular kind of greed.

If the TM® goal is enlightenment, which is what the movement would like us to believe, and if the movement believes as Maharishi teaches that all seven states of consciousness have corresponding physiological correlates, and if Maharishi is indeed at least in CC (if not UC), then why hasn't any research been performed on Maharishi himself? Whose psychophysiology would be better suited? Wouldn't this enlighten the world about the truth behind these claims? Or are we to accept on blind faith that these seven states of consciousness do indeed exist outside the theoretical realm? Apparently so!

During my six years with the movement I never heard reports of any scientific proof of any states of consciousness other than waking, dreaming and sleeping. Dr. R. Keith Wallace, a TM® researcher who himself practices TM® and is now president of Maharishi International University, proposed on the basis of his research that there is a fourth major state of consciousness which he terms "restful alertness." Even if this proposed state were to become generally accepted by the scientific and medical community, it would not provide any evidence in support of Maharishi's thesis about the path of development from sleeping to unity consciousness.

The reason I say this is that Maharishi talks about TC (transcendental consciousness—those moments during TM® when there is no mantra and no thought, and yet you aren't asleep) as being the basis for growth to CC. Those moments of "transcending" have not yet been physiologically defined. What *has* been theoretically defined (if we can trust the scientific evidence collected to date) is the overall experience of TM® which involves, for the most part, daydreaming mixed with the mantra and very infrequent moments of blank mind. This is the subjective experience of the proposed state of restful alertness, and even that hypothesis is being seriously challenged now, as described in Appendix 5.

So if Maharishi wants us to believe the story of psychophysiological correlates to each of the four states of consciousness which he proposes as being sequentially beyond sleeping, dreaming and waking, then we will need some hard scientific proof of the tangible existence of this fourth state known as "transcendental consciousness" or, more simply, "transcending." In the absence of this proof, we are again in the position of having to believe Maharishi's claim to be sole holder of the "the truth of life."

I never once met an individual who claimed to have attained CC, GC (refined CC) or UC. We had all been told that if a person reached CC, he wouldn't want to make it publicly known because people might be tempted into some form of hero-worship of the individual. Another reason is that a person wouldn't be able to have any privacy. People would be after him all the time with questions about what CC was like. At least this was Maharishi's explanation for why we would never know CC until we reached it ourselves, and also why it would never become public information if someone attained CC.

Remember, a person in CC will show no outward signs of having changed. The only difference will be in his "level of perception." Since

1. I never met anyone who claimed to be in CC, and
2. Maharishi has said that an individual would never publicize the fact that he or she achieved CC, and
3. Maharishi did claim that there are people in CC,

we are led to rely totally on Maharishi's word that the CC story is true.

One more piece of information you should be aware of is this: Maharishi defines CC psychophysiologically as the state of consciousness which results from a stress-free nervous system. According to him, once a person gains CC, he will no longer accumulate stress. CC also forms the basis for any of the proposed higher states of consciousness.

Maharishi also read and approved the bestseller *TM** by Harold Bloomfield, Michael Cain and Dennis Jaffe. Keep in mind that Maharishi personally endorsed as accurate the statements about his teachings and beliefs. We find on page 213 of the Dell edition of *TM**:

> *All of us are familiar with the extent to which our society reflects individual dishonesty, manipulation, fear, anger, frustration, prejudice and hatred. The clear indication of the evidence presented in this*

book, however, is that these characteristics result from individual stress and are not intrinsic to the self.

Bloomfield *et al.* emphasize that
1. Dishonesty results from individual stress, and
2. Manipulation results from individual stress.

With respect to the first point, dishonesty is defined as "Characterized by falsehood or *intent to mislead.*"Maharishi has claimed that the selection of mantras is systematic. We have proof that it is random and that he intentionally misled his followers into believing the hoax in order to have them carry his schemes abroad.

With respect to the second point, manipulation is defined as "To manage shrewdly and deviously *for one's own profit.*" Maharishi and his movement have obviously profited from his shrewd management of the above-mentioned deception, as well as from the puja cover-up.

We therefore come to the conclusion, based on Maharishi's own analysis of the source of the two qualities (dishonesty and manipulation), that Maharishi must still be subject to the scourge of individual stress.

If this is the case, then according to his earlier definition of CC and higher states of consciousness, Maharishi could in no way be in any other state of consciousness than normal wakingness except when he is asleep or dreaming. Or if the state of restful alertness is a reality and if TM® does produce the proper conditions for its existence, then possibly, if Maharishi practices what he preaches, at least with respect to the TM® technique, he also would attain the state of restful alertness on occasion. But could he be in CC, GC or UC? Not by his current definitions. By logical analysis based on his own definitions, Maharishi could not be enlightened—unless he has other definitions for dishonesty and manipulation.

We can assume, then, that no change in actions or personality would accompany being enlightened, which is what Maharishi has stated. For example, suppose a military man began meditation at the beginning of a war and he fought in it for eight years, during which time he continued to meditate regularly, releasing stress and then finally "dropping into CC." Would he still continue fighting and killing, except that he would just be a "witness to himself" as he gunned down fellow humans? Would he now feel fulfilled within himself and no longer overshadowed by his perceptions of the human slaughter and indignities around him? Maharishi has never spoken out against war during any talks I heard him give. On the other hand, I have heard him glorifying the U.S. military for their enlightened acceptance of TM® into its ranks. The inference is that Maharishi tacitly defines enlightenment as the state of agreement with whatever Maharishi says or does.

In any case, for those who do believe him, he's holding out the bait, whetting their appetites and building in them a strong lust for CC and higher states of consciousness. Here is the spiritual greed that will drive them to do almost anything Maharishi asks, orders or even hints at. If it is Maharishi's will, meditators figure, then it will only serve to bring us that much closer to CC. Maharishi's tight-lipped attitude about providing tangible evidence for the existence of CC leads his followers into a merry-go-round of assumptions about why he won't tell us everything. The attitude grows that fosters thoughts such as "Maybe Paul's in CC" or "Is Eileen in CC?" or "I heard a rumor that so-and-so just hit it!"

Maharishi's vagueness, combined with his apparent "leaks" of the "truth" about CC, leads some people to develop a smug sense of "I must be pretty special to have caught *that* particular secret." It is as if Maharishi speaks in a code at times which can only be understood by people who are more evolved. Also, his occasional moments of finally bringing the truth about a particular topic out into the open leads to the necessity of sticking close to his movement in order not to miss the next esoteric truth. The belief is that Maharishi is only permitting us to know that which will be useful to us now, that as more and more people reach higher levels of evolution, he will begin to unfold the "truth" about those higher levels. Maharishi's entire movement revolves around this faith in his supposed omniscience. So we hear people saying things like "Next course he's going to tell the truth about the Brahma Sutras' hidden meanings regarding celestial vision" or "Did you hear about Brahman Consciousness? It's one step beyond Unity!" No proof is ever given, no proof is ever demanded.

So for those who get absorbed into this miasma of pseudospirituality, the desire for CC or higher is pervasive and, for many, all-consuming. The only solution to this unsatisfied hunger is to obey the words of the "master," who says that the quickest way to CC is to teach TM®. The puja is the "highway," Maharishi claims. It's a nonstop expressway to cosmic consciousness. For example, we find this statement on page 2 in the Introduction to *The Holy Tradition:*

> This increasing ability of maintaining deeper awareness and at the same time, speech and action on the surface, is a direct path to the development of Cosmic Consciousness. This is how, when the initiator is leading the new initiate into Transcendental Consciousness, he himself is rising into Cosmic Consciousness. This explains why and how the initiator feels more and more surcharged with increasing degree of Cosmic Consciousness. That means more energy, more intelligence, more happiness, more freedom from bondage, more liberation, and more fulfillment.

Note here the qualities defined as being the hallmarks of CC: energy, intelligence, happiness, freedom from bondage, liberation and fulfillment. Picture Hitler being described in these terms by his followers. Movement people would be quick to say that Hitler's followers actually experienced *false* happiness, *false* liberation, etc., but that's not the case with us. Or is it? When you "buy into" TM®, you throw your discrimination away and enter a pervasive mood around the movement that causes an automatic "Good" button to light up in your head— whether meditator or teacher—whenever

82

you hear CC mentioned. As I look back on it now, it's almost frightening to think how easily I was taken in with the flowery words and the flowery presence of Maharishi.

And yet given the world conditions today, it's not really so difficult to understand why people are attracted to Maharishi's promises. He pledges great solutions in vague terms which allow wide latitude for personal interpretation, and he comes through with an immediate reward of relaxation if you buy into the game. You're led to believe that since his first promise of deep rest was fulfilled, why not all the rest of the claims? By the time you catch yourself thinking again, you find you're headed toward the honeypot of CC with many other fellow idealists. And if you continue long enough, you eventually graduate to "exponent of reality" as I did, leading still more people into Maharishi's spiritual trap.

As we have already seen in Maharishi's description of the qualities of CC, the state of CC is not necessarily "good" in the accepted sense of a moral "good" as opposed to a moral "bad." However, for some reason, when I as an initiator heard the promise of CC, I thought "good." As a result, it seemed logical to expect that as an individual grew in "increasing degrees of cosmic consciousness," as Maharishi describes the developmental process, the implication was strong that there should be increasing evidence of greater love and human concern among initiators in particular, but also between the initiators and the people in the world whom we were there to "enlighten" with our wisdom.

On numerous occasions, however, I was surprised to see examples of just the opposite attitude developing. The public face of a TM® teacher was always the picture of sincerity and wholesomeness, but behind closed doors the story was quite different. For instance, on many of the teacher training courses that I attended for rest and rounding as an initiator, the common setup was to have an "initiators' dining hall" and a "meditators' dining hall." This segregation was based on the movement hierarchy of least-stressed people to the most-stressed people. The stressed-out meditators who were "unstressing like crazy" on their way to becoming more highly evolved and purified initiators were expected to eat apart from the poor, tired initiators who needed their peace and quiet for the more mature concerns of the upper echelon members of the TM® movement.

This was a commonly accepted feeling among many, many initiators, though it would be unfair to say all. However, this spiritual pride was supported by the structure of the movement and by Maharishi himself. Maharishi has based much of his current teachings on this statement: "Knowledge is structured in consciousness." By this he means that a person's level of consciousness determines the structure and quality of his understanding. What that person does or says or creates is therefore an expression of his level of consciousness.

The TM® movement is obviously Maharishi's creation, so we can say that it is an expression of his level of consciousness. If the TM® movement's structure supports spiritual pride and spiritual greed, then those qualities must be elements in Maharishi's own level of consciousness.

The element of spiritual pride carries over to the workaday world of the initiators in the field, working through TM® centers in cities and towns across the country and around the world. The initiator builds up the local area meditators into believing that close contact with the organization will lead to a quicker development of CC for that person. Then the initiator through this process creates a corps of "helpers" who essentially serve the functions of errand-runners and stamp-lickers. I don't want to generalize unfairly, so I must point out that at the local level, dishonesty and deception may not be an actively functioning element in the TM® process. The initiator, who is unaware of the material covered in Chapter 3, may for the most part be acting in good faith throughout all of his or her teaching activities. The meditator who enjoys the experience and yet knows absolutely nothing, in truth, about what he or she is involved in may be, and usually is, helping out just because it's fun or because he sincerely wants to be of service—not for spiritual greed.

However, the element of spiritual greed is built into the process of becoming an initiator and is, in fact, an integral part of the structure of the movement. If you move far enough into the movement, you can't avoid it. Every time initiators perform the puja during initiation, they are reminded of the "fact" that they are rushing on to the ocean of CC while the initiate is just dipping his toes into the pond of TC. Maharishi even emphasized this point during teacher training as one of the main trade secrets of the teaching process. He would say, "We always get more than the initiate, but we never let them know this is the case." Thus Maharishi is supporting and even creating through this teaching a strong attitude of greed, false pride and arrogance which is not becoming to people who are supposedly rushing to enlightenment.

It was March, 1973. The setting was a private home in Hartford, Connecticut. A group of initiators and local meditators were having a get-together following the first one-day SCI Businessmen's Symposium at Renssalear Polytechnic Institute, which had just ended. It had been a long, full and exciting day. Several hundred local business people had turned out for the symposium. It was billed as a presentation of a new concept in improving the business community's quality of life through the introduction of the Science of Creative Intelligence into their programs for personnel improvement, employee-management relations, etc.

The idea for such a symposium was very sensible. The TM® movement wanted to reach the business community, and symposiums are a generally accepted form of communication within the business world. The material that was presented was basically an elaborate introductory TM® lecture geared for the business world. You could hear pretty much the same stuff if you went to the first free lecture open to the public. Nevertheless, the idea seemed like a sound one, and many attendees left feeling well-informed about the TM® program. Dr. Glueck from the Institute of Living had presented some of his preliminary research results and had impressed many people in the audience with his informative presentation. Other locally-known speakers gave testimonials, and on the whole it was a great success.

When I arrived at the post-symposium party, I walked into the kitchen and found two of my good initiator friends talking. They had been instrumental in setting up the symposium. One is now a high official in the movement and has authored or co-authored several well-known books about TM®. As I approached I heard the following dialogue.

"Isn't it amazing?"

"It's incredible!"

"It wasn't anything more than an introductory lecture!"

"I know. And the really incredible thing is that we got them to *pay* for it!"

"Amazing."

"Isn't it?"

I was shocked. I had felt it was pretty nice that the people at the symposium had been given an opportunity to hear about TM®. I thought that TM® could be of value to many of the people who had come, if not to all.

I left the party a few minutes later and went home. That evening was one of the first run-ins I had with my conscience about the inherent goodness of TM®. One of those teachers had been meditating for more than four years when that conversation took place. The other had been meditating for approximately three years. Yet it appeared that these "spiritually advanced" meditators were more excited about having deceived a group of people into paying to hear what was essentially an introductory lecture they could otherwise hear for free than to have had the opportunity to share the "truth of life" with fellow human beings.

"You shall know them by their fruits," the Bible tells us. Spiritual greed, spiritual pride, arrogance, manipulation, deceit and dishonesty seem to be, for openers, a list of the fruits of TM®. Maharishi's "expressway to enlightenment" doesn't seem to be very well marked on the roadmap of morality.

Chapter Seven

MANTRAS: THE GODS OF TM®

Shortly after becoming an initiator, I taught a weekend residence course with another initiator in Litchfield, Connecticut. As I was browsing through a book shelf at the facility, I found a book by Ravi Kumar entitled *Tantra Asana* (Wittenborn Publishers: New York, 1971). It was a large, hardbound collection of painting and photographs of sculptures from the Tantric tradition. According to the book, Tantra is an eastern path of self-realization that somehow unites the "earthly" with the "transcendental" through various methods.

I opened to the first page and found a painting of a human form. On the facing page was the following text:

AING, AING is Thy favorite mantra,
Thou who art both form and formlessness,
Who art the wealth of the lotus face of the lotus-born,
Embodiment of all gunas, yet devoid of attributes,
Changeless, and neither gross nor subtle.

Aing—that was my mantra! And it was written in bold letters on the opening page of a book about an Indian religious tradition. Moreover, this mantra apparently was the favorite one of the object of that exhortation. As I looked further into the book, it seemed to be a highly esoteric form of worship of certain Hindu gods.

That was quite a shocking experience for me; I felt as if I had just been caught reading a dirty book. A lot of questions about this experience of seeing my mantra in print, particularly in the context of Tantra worship, came to mind. But I didn't pursue them at the time. I simply filed the data away in my memory for future reference.

Later that year (summer, 1971) I attended a one-month course at the University of Massachusetts in Amherst for rest and rounding. The initiator refresher course was being held in conjunction with a teacher training course for meditators. I met with Maharishi privately during that course to receive his authorization to become an initiator of adults.

During that meeting I also received my third advanced technique. This was the next in the advanced techniques series. I had received my "night technique" described in Chapter 2 and assumed that this time I would receive an addition to my current mantra or perhaps a new mantra. I was curious since I had seen that the mantra I was using was part of an esoteric form of worship in another tradition. Maharishi had said on many occasions that in "our meditation," by which he meant TM®, the mantras were meaningless—only serving the purpose of allowing our minds to settle within easily and effortlessly. There was in no way any meaning attributed to the mantra, particularly not of any religious significance.

As I knelt at Maharishi's bedside, he asked me to whisper my mantra to him. I closed my eyes and thought it to myself easily, and then whispered, "Aaing."

"Very good," he said. Then he paused and said, "From now on your mantra will be . . . *namah.*" He instructed me to say it softly, which I did. Then he had me try a brief meditation of about a minute with it while I sat on the floor.

At that point I felt confused. If you recall the chapter on

the puja ceremony, I already knew that the English meaning of *namah* is "I bow down." Maharishi obviously knew that I understood the meaning of *namah*. "Maybe," I thought, "he thinks I don't know about the *Aaing* part of it." I honestly didn't know what to make of the circumstance. I had been publicly proclaiming in the name of Maharishi that the mantras didn't have any meaning and that TM® was not in conflict with any religious beliefs. Now that I knew the truth about the mantras and also the advanced techniques, was I expected to continue with these deceptive teachings?

I felt like a fool, but I haltingly asked Maharishi what was going on. I told him about reading *Tantra Asana* and the apparent use of *Aaing* to worship a deity, and that he was now giving me a mental expression for bowing down to this deity Aaing. I waited for a reply, but none came.

I began to feel very uncomfortable as the silence continued. Maharishi then made a statement to the effect that he didn't quite understand my question—that there were many more people waiting to see him, so I should hurry along and scoot out the door. Looking back on that confrontation, I can see that I was apparently expected to be ecstatic over having the truth about the deception revealed to me. He was including me in his real inner circle and I was supposed to show reverence for this generous act. At the time I was near the end of another bout of rounding and was therefore, in the movement's terms, in no condition to take anything too seriously since I was "obviously" unstressing very heavily. Like a dutiful soldier, I buried the memory of that experience in my mental basement and went back upstairs.

It was one and a half years later, during the spring of 1973, that I received my fourth technique. It turned out to be nothing more than adding the word *Shri* (often spelled *Sri)* to the beginning of my then-current mantra, *Aaing namah.* So my new mantra at the end of four years of practicing Transcendental Meditation was *Shri Aaing namah.* Translated into English, this mantra made the statement, "O most beautiful Aaing, I bow down to you."

Shortly after the course I happened to come across a book by the French scholar Alain Danielou entitled *Hindu Polytheism* (Bollingen Foundation: Princeton, 1964). The chapter concerned with mantras is entitled "The Thought-Forms, or Mantras." Of what were the mantras thought-forms? According to Danielou, a recognized Indologist, they are thoughtforms of Hindu gods and goddesses, and their main use is in worship of the various deities in the Hindu pantheon. A mantra is described as a "seed-utterance" of a particular deity. In simpler terms, a mantra is a code-name for a deity. In addition to listing the mantras and identifying the deity that the mantra refers to, Danielou describes the benefits said to be gained from worshipping that particular deity.

I was most interested to see if any of the mantras which Maharishi employed in his teaching were included in the chapter. Here was an opportunity to put some of the pieces of Maharishi's mystery puzzle together. As I read on in the chapter, I found that only one of the mantras listed and described was from Maharishi's teachings. It was not until 1973, after my wife and I discussed our mutual growing doubts about TM®, that I learned there were other mantras used in TM®. At that time I looked at *Hindu Polytheism* again and saw that of the six mantras listed, Maharishi was actually using four. They are spelled *Aim, Hrim, Srim* and *Krim* by Danielou, but they are the same ones that Maharishi spelled more phonetically as *Aem, Hirim, Shirim* and *Kirim*.

At the time, *Aim* was the only mantra, of the ones listed, with which I was familiar. Danielou states that *Aim* is also called Sarasvata or Sarasvati, which means "pertaining to the goddess of knowledge." So the goddess of knowledge, Sarasvati, the consort of Brahma, is worshipped with the mantra *Aim*. We find in the Invocation section of *The Holy Tradition* that the spirit of Lord Shankaracharya is invoked in the name of Brahmananda *Saraswati* during the performance of the puja.

There seems to be a link between the deities invoked

during the performance of the puja and their code-names or mantras. By the way, "invocation" means: 1. the act of invoking or appealing to a deity or other agent for help, inspiration, witness, etc.; 2. a prayer; 3. an appeal for assistance to the Muses or some divine being; 4. the act of conjuring an evil spirit; 5. the words or incantation used.

If a link does exist between the mantras of TM® and the puja ceremony, it would certainly begin to explain the statement by Jerry Jarvis that the mantras will not work unless they are imparted in conjunction with the puja. In other words, the puja would theoretically invite various deities to the immediate vicinity, thereby creating the "active atmosphere" described on page 3 of *The Holy Tradition:*

> *The making of the offerings enriches the active atmosphere with the bliss of silence and enlivens the quietness of the area with sublime and blissful activity. . . . A calm wave of spiritual influence is generated. . . .*

And then once the deities are present and have received the devotional offerings, one of them is singled out by the initiator when he assigns the mantra to the initiate.

But if we accept the claim that the mantras are only meaningless sounds whose vibratory effects are known, then it would not make sense that the puja was an absolute prerequisite for the effective teaching of the mantras as Jerry Jarvis has stated. If the mantras in and of themselves contain certain secular and scientific vibrational qualities, why should an invocation of various Hindu deities be necessary to get the mantras functioning properly?

In support of this view that there is a link between the mantras and the puja, Maharishi has given an affirmative reply to the question, "Are the gods we bow down to in the puja the same as the mantras?" This question was asked by a meditator to Maharishi in La Antilla, Spain during the teacher training course which my wife attended in the spring of 1973. It was asked in an assembly of all the trainees, so there are hundreds of witnesses to the veracity of this statement.

It seems that the religious nature of Maharishi's program carries over from the practice of the puja to the actual practice of the meditation. In other words, the TM® movement's claim of non-conflict with other religions is not supported by any elements in Maharishi's teachings. A Christian, for example, which is what I profess to be, would commit a serious act of false worship even through the "innocent" act of sitting down to meditate twice a day.

Maharishi is extremely shrewd and clever. Here is an example of how well he has covered his tracks. A young initiator, Chris Meade, who went so far as to meditate for four years and to attend a five-month teacher training course, never realized the extent of his religious involvement in Maharishi's program. In the *Oberlin Alumni Magazine,* March-April 1976, Chris explained his feeling of guilt about deceiving people into believing that TM® didn't conflict with other religions.

> Most pointedly I felt guilty for having to tell people that TM® conflicted with no religions. *While the actual practice of the technique—apart from initiation—had little to do with other faiths,* the tantalizing promises we made as initiators were almost equal to guaranteeing divinity to all meditators—or, at the very least, sainthood. (Emphasis mine)

After four years of meditation Chris still did not realize he was unknowingly worshipping some Hindu deity during meditation. (He stopped practicing TM® anyway six months after he became a teacher.) Does a regular meditator off the street receive the same "advanced techniques" as initiators? In other words, are the obvious religious aspects of the advanced technique which I received, the *namah* and the *shri,* only included in an initiator's advanced techniques since only an initiator would be able to understand what those words denote? This would be part of the process of making the initiator feel more a part of the "inner circle."

If a meditator has no access to an English-Sanskrit dictionary, he would never be able to unlock the hidden meanings of the "meaningless mantras" unless he had experienced the sort of unintentional discoveries I had made. So if those same advanced techniques are given to meditators who have not joined the ranks of the initiators, the deception is grossly magnified. Also, the intentionality of the act of deception becomes sorely apparent. Are these same techniques given to non-initiators? The answer is— Yes. A young woman I know who originally had been given the mantra *Aim* in 1971 was given as her new mantra, upon receiving her advanced technique, *Aaing namah.* Since the initiators who receive the advanced techniques have at least a chance of realizing what they are involved in, why aren't the meditators given the same advantage? Why aren't they made aware of the devotional nature of the practice, particularly if this devotion is supposedly such a positive and wonderful part of the growth to higher states of consciousness? The answer is obvious.

Thus far we have found that:

1. Mantras do indeed have meanings.
2. Mantras are code-names for various Hindu deities.
3. The act of meditating is a form of Hindu sacred worship (but it occurs in other religions as well, of course).

The TM® movement, however, claims that the only meanings of the mantras lie in their very special "vibrational qualities" which no other sounds possess. We are not told what these qualities are. It seems likely that the vibrational qualities are those vibrations most pleasing to a particular deity or god.

The TM® movement will reply, "You may call it a god. We say that's just a primitive, ignorant and nonscientific understanding of the term 'vibrational quality' or 'vibration'."

The term "god" may be primitive in some people's world

view, but the TM® movement's alternative definition of a mantra is found to be almost identical to the dictionary definition of a "god." On page 43 of *TM**, which was fully approved by Maharishi, mantras are defined as follows: "Mantra is a Sanskrit term which designates 'a thought the effects of which are known' not on the level of meaning—in fact the mantras taught for use in the TM® technique have no denotative meaning—but on the level of vibratory effect, analogous to sound quality."

Compare that with the *Reader's Digest Encyclopedic Dictionary* definition of "god": "One of various beings . . . conceived of as immortal . . . as embodying a particular quality or principle, as personifying or controlling a particular element or phenomenon of nature, or as having special powers or influence over some phase of life." The "vibratory effect which is known" concept is easily equatable with "quality controlling a particular element of nature," and is an example of how the movement plays with words and concepts to fool the public. It is widely understood within the movement that mantras are supposed to have special powers or influences over some phase of life. This is why they are said to be selected on the basis of a meditator's special psychological make-up, to be just right for the "subtle differences" between one person and another.

For the sake of discussion, let's concede the point about the mantra being "just a vibration." In that case, why do we have to "bow down" *(namah)* to the "most beautiful" *(shri)* vibrational quality? Call it what you will—vibrational quality, power of nature, bestower of prosperity, or a god— this phrase is a form of devotional worship.

At this point, any reasonable person must agree, the argument that TM® is not religious falls apart completely. But don't assume that all meditators and initiators are reasonable. I was all too typical of the irrational believer constituting the TM® movement. When people want to believe something, they find any excuse, however fabricated or fantastic, to justify their course of action and to rationalize away their doubts and guilts.

Someone might ask, "If the meditator isn't aware of the meaning of his mantra, how could his meditation be called religious?" If we look to the source of the mantras, the Hindu religion, we find that with these sounds the various deities are worshipped. Belief in those deities isn't required for the worship to be effected. Simply the utterance of the sound—speaking the mantra—effects the act of worship. And the TM® movement supports this by claiming that the effectiveness of the vibratory quality of these sounds does not require any belief, and that the mantras work independently of any belief or faith in them.

The TM® movement also claims that the mantras serve only one function, which is described on page 44 of *TM** like this: ". . . to effect the spontaneous process of reducing mental activity during practice of the TM® technique." If so, why then do the authors go on to explain the importance of using only TM®-approved mantras (instead of finding one in a Hindu text, or even making up one's own nonmeaningful sound) on the basis of the results of the meditative experience? The widely-used Sanskrit mantra *Om,* we are told by the TM® movement, leads one into a reclusive life. The TM® mantras, on the other hand, lead to expansive material growth and an outgoing attitude.

Apparently the function of the mantra is more involved than the claim of simply reducing mental activity during meditation. It seems that certain effects are created in a person's life as a result of using a particular mantra in addition to the mantra serving its alleged function of reducing mental activity during TM® meditation. In other words, it is not just the reduction of mental activity which is important to the technique's results. It is the *combination* of this reduced activity along with the mantra's other effects that brings the results. The movement places far more emphasis on the importance of the mantra itself than it does on the importance of transcending through the reduction of mental activity. Mantras are not, after all, the only way to reduce mental activity.

The warning is given by the movement that the use of non-approved mantras can lead to harmful results, such as headaches, anxiety and disrupted attention span. Chris Meade described his feelings after a five-month experience of regularly using his TM®-approved mantra many hours each day and with the guidance of Maharishi himself always available. Quoting a letter he wrote to his parents at that time, he said:

> *"The basic thing I have seen is that I seem to have lost (temporarily I hope) that easygoing pervasive happiness that was building up for the last year or so, and in its place is a fundamental, almost atavistic confusion." The confusion persisted throughout the course, and was at times very painful, but I bore with it because I believed it to be unstressing. Surprisingly, though, after the course (when I was a full initiator), the confusion did not leave.*

Later in his article Chris added:

> *Despite my troubled state of mind, I continued to meditate regularly for more than six months after the course was over. I kept on waiting for the "unstressing" to end, and for me to feel completely the expanded state of consciousness that was promised me. I asked older initiators what was taking so long and they said things like, "Maybe you should go to another course" or "Sometimes it takes quite a long time to see how far we really have advanced in consciousness."*

Chris's experience is far from unique. It is also mild in comparison to many other unfortunate meditation casualties of the TM® movement's "progressive forward march."

Meditators have been lied to on many occasions throughout their contact with the TM® movement, and the deception about mantras is one of the more insidious lies. The TM® movement is structured in such a way that a person can begin the practice of TM® with the understanding that:

1. The TM® technique is not religious.
2. A meaningless sound is the basis of the technique.
3. A secular ceremony of gratitude is performed during instruction.
4. The student is not required to participate in the ceremony.

We have learned the following information so far:

1. The puja ceremony is clearly religious.
2. The mantras are also religious.
3. The mantras are not meaningless. They are the code-names of Hindu deities and provide the means for worshipping those deities.
4. The puja ceremony is clearly identified as an invocation of "the Holy Tradition," so it is not merely a secular expression of gratitude.
5. The student is definitely a participant in the ceremony. He provides the fruit, flowers and handkerchief used in the ceremony, and must take part in both word and deed if he wishes to be initiated.
6. Maharishi has admitted that the mantras are representative of the same gods worshipped and invoked during the puja.
7. The gods will in turn supply the worshipper with numerous material benefits and rewards in return for the devotional act of bowing down and giving worship to them in both the puja and the meditation itself.
8. Jerry Jarvis has said that the mantras will not work without the puja being performed before they are imparted.

In light of these facts, I will propose in the next chapter an alternative explanation of an important aspect of the TM® program's teaching, namely, the meaning of unstressing.

Chapter Eight

UNWELCOME VISITORS:
TM® AND DEMONIC POSSESSION—I

Jabez Stone received a tremendous amount of publicity in the late 1930's when a short story by Stephen Vincent Benet appeared in the *Saturday Evening Post*. At that time transcendental meditation was unknown, but stress and strain were well known by all.

What had Jabez done to deserve such attention? As Benet told it, Jabez Stone sold his soul to the devil. Stone's wife was ailing, his two children were down with the measles, and his horse was sick. When his plowshare broke on a stone in his rocky field, in a fit of frustration he vowed that not only was his predicament enough to warrant selling his soul, but that he would be quite willing to do it on the spot for just two cents.

The long and the short of it is that the next evening "Old Scratch" himself arrived and closed the deal in proper business fashion. From that day forth Jabez's luck took a turn for the better, and for the next seven years nothing went wrong. All aspects of his life improved two hundred per cent. He was the envy of the neighborhood. As far as anyone could tell from external appearances, the Stone family had found the key to a fulfilled life. And no one but Jabez knew the real reason until his debt to Mr. Scratch came due for payment in the seventh year. At that point, in fear of eternal damnation, Stone called upon the aid of Daniel Webster, the greatest trial lawyer of the time, to win back his soul.

"The Devil and Daniel Webster" is a well-loved classic in America's literary heritage. As far as we can tell, it is nothing more than a fictitious legend relating some commonly accepted notions about how the devil deals his deck, and how an honest-hearted and courageous man was able to beat the devil at his own game.

How did Jabez Stone feel during the first few years after he made his bargain? As Benet tells it, Jabez felt pretty good: ". . . when bad luck turns, it drives most other things out of your head."

A number of points came to mind after recently re-reading Benet's story:

— The devil is usually thought to be a very slick gentleman.

— People everywhere readily accept the notion that physical and material blessings are trademarks of the devil's work.

— The business of selling one's soul to the devil is not elaborate or complex but actually quite effortless.

— The business of winning Jabez's soul back from the devil demanded unabashed honesty and an appeal to basic human concerns on the part of Daniel Webster.

The *Reader's Digest Encyclopedic Dictionary* defines "devil" as:

1. In Jewish and Christian theology, the prince and ruler of the kingdom of evil; Satan.
2. Any subordinate evil spirit; a demon.
3. In Christian Science usage, evil; a lie; error; . . . opposite of Truth; . . . or hypnotism.

And from the Bible we find in John 8:44:

You are of your father the devil, and your will is to do

your father's desires. He was a murderer from the
beginning, and has nothing to do with the truth,
because there is no truth in him. When he lies, he
speaks according to his own nature, for he is a liar and
the father of lies.

And yet, as we see in II Corinthians 11:14-15, the devil's appearance will not be indicative of anything ungodly or covert:

And no wonder, for even Satan disguises himself as
an angel of light. So it is not strange if his servants
also disguise themselves as servants of righteousness.

The TM® movement's public image is nothing less than pure and righteous. The promises of the TM® movement are almost equal to guarantees of divinity to all practitioners of the technique, if not sainthood, as Chris Meade so nicely puts it. And the promised relaxation *is* produced. However, despite the fact that the material and physical blessings of relaxation and greater energy are produced by TM®, the entire TM® movement and the TM® teachings are founded on dishonesty and deceptive practices. Perhaps the spiritual source of the TM® movement *might not* be the light of God, but rather an angel of light.

The clearest description of demons and their influences is to be found in the Bible. For that reason—and also because demonology is one of the secret teachings of the TM® movement—we'll spend some time examining the movement's concept of unstressing. We will do this with reference to the Bible.

The suggestion that there may be a relationship between TM® and demonic or Satanic influences has been proposed by Gordon Lewis, a professor of systematic theology and Christian philosophy, in his book *What Everyone Should Know About Transcendental Meditation* (Regal Books: Glendale, California, 1975). Lewis' book deals for the most part with information that is readily available to the public from Maharishi's teachings and the TM® movement. His analysis of the teachings from a Christian perspective leads

Lewis to several conclusions, including:

> *TM propaganda must be considered in the light of . . . the apostle Paul's* [explanation] *that it may be worship and service of the creature more than the Creator, and Satan's deceptive power to change himself into an angel of light.*

This conclusion was drawn without knowledge of the meaning of the mantras, the deceptive tactics of the TM® movement, or the understanding of the true significance of the puja ceremony. Lewis based his argument solely on statements about the TM® philosophy as publicly disseminated by the movement.

I will approach the possibility of a connection between TM® and demonic forces from three viewpoints. The first will be a consideration of whether there is biblical support for it. The second will be a comparison of the TM® experience with the experiences of spiritists, mediums and occultists. The third will be an account of experiences of meditators themselves. (In one case a girl I know claimed quite seriously that a demonic being entered her body by jumping down her throat and taking possession of her while she was meditating.)

A few years ago, David, a good friend who had been initiated into TM®, decided, on the basis of his study of the Bible, that he no longer wanted to be associated with the TM® movement. His wife felt the same way. Since they no longer practiced TM, they didn't want to be part of the movement's statistics.*

---

*The movement's statistics are highly deceptive and misleading. I estimate, on the basis of my years as a local initiator, that the number of people who discontinue practicing TM® is roughly fifty per cent. When the movement announces that there are now 750,000 or 1,000,000 people meditating, it really means that many people were initiated and paid their course fee. No records are kept of those who stop meditating. For example, my wife and I no longer meditate, yet we are counted as part of the meditating population by the TM® movement.

This brings into serious question the claims of the movement in a recent study attempting to relate a decrease in crime to the practice of

Dave and his wife lived near Philadelphia at the time and were on the mailing list of the Philadelphia SIMS center, so they called SIMS there and asked to have their names removed from the records. The initiator on the other end of the wire wanted to know why they had decided to stop meditating. When Dave explained that their decision was based on an attempt to apply biblical principles to their daily lives—principles that would not permit them to blindly follow the teachings of a man who didn't seem to be in harmony with the Bible—the initiator replied, "But TM® isn't religious. It doesn't conflict with anything in the Bible. As a matter of fact, Jesus Christ was the first transcendental meditator."

What could that TM® teacher have been thinking of when he made that statement? In the same breath he was denying his own "Holy Tradition" and making false statements about Jesus and the Bible. The "ancient Holy Tradition" which has supposedly maintained the "systematic procedure for choosing mantras" has been around since 5000 B.C., according to the movement. Perhaps the initiator was not aware that the term "B.C." means "before Christ." Or perhaps the initiator had a momentary lapse of memory about the source of his trade. Or perhaps—and probably more likely—the initiator felt that Dave was just unstressing, was deluded, or had been misguided by some ignorant teachings in the Bible and that he could set Dave straight by saying *anything* to appeal to Dave's misguided concern about making an *effort* (though according to Maharishi, effort isn't required for anything worthwhile!) to lead his life in accordance with the Word of God.

TM®. They claim that in ten cities across the country where more than one per cent of the population meditate, the crime rate decreased compared to the previous year's crime rate. But since no records are kept of those who stop meditating, the experimental design for this crime study is totally inadequate. If one per cent of the population of a town is initiated, that does not mean they are meditating. Probably no more than half of them are.

As I have shown in previous chapters, there is irreconcilable conflict between the teachings of Jesus and the teachings of Maharishi. Jesus did not teach transcendental meditation. He never taught His followers to sit comfortably with their eyes closed and mentally repeat the names of Hindu deities to themselves. He never taught His followers to spread the good news of the Kingdom of God through deceitful tactics. He never said that faith was not required to gain God's favor, as we find the TM® movement is so strongly proclaiming.

Maharishi teaches that God is only interested in knowing us when we have eliminated all the stress from our bodies through the faithless, effortless, nonreligious practice of TM®. Maharishi also teaches that one of the benefits of TM® is a spontaneous ability to perform right action, implying the ability to determine right from wrong just like God. Jesus never taught that we should come to know right from wrong spontaneously. That ability belongs only to God. In order for us to know right from wrong, we must examine the Scriptures daily to make sure we are acting in accordance with the divine will of God. Even then, due to our human imperfection, we will continue to make errors. In other words, Jesus did not teach that we should be striving to become equal to God in order to "know Him" or gain His favor. As we see in Philippians 2:5-6,

> *Have this mind among yourselves, which you have in Christ Jesus, who, though He was in the form of God, did not count equality with God a thing to be grasped . . .*

We can safely conclude that Jesus did not practice TM® either. His prayers to His Father in heaven were not quiet mental repetitions of a Sanskrit thoughtform of the Hindu goddess Sarasvati, consort of Brahma, or any other thoughtform or code name of a polytheistic deity. His prayers were directed to His father in heaven "whose name is YHWH [Yahweh, Jehovah] forever," as stated in Exodus

3:15. Moreover, his prayers were very meaningful semantically—not just on the level of "vibration."

If Jesus did not teach or practice TM®, then it could not be a divine teaching from God. Is there any indication from the Bible where such a teaching might have originated? Yes, there is.

We find that the originator of this teaching of "becoming like God" and spontaneously knowing right from wrong or good from evil is introduced in the third chapter of Genesis. In Genesis 3:4-5 we find:

> *But the serpent said to the woman, "You will not die. For God knows that when you eat of it your eyes will be opened, and you will be like God, knowing good and evil.*

The serpent is identified in numerous other places throughout the Bible as being one and the same as the Devil and Satan. Most clearly we find this in Revelation 12:9:

> *And the great dragon was thrown down, that ancient serpent, who is called the Devil and Satan, the deceiver of the whole world . . .*

Some of the distinguishing characteristics of the false apostles whose teachings have their source in satanic quarters are described in II Corinthians 11:3-4, 12-15:

> *But I am afraid that as the serpent deceived Eve by his cunning, your thoughts will be led astray from a sincere and pure devotion to Christ. For if some one comes and preaches another Jesus than the one we preached, or if you receive a different spirit from the one you received, or if you accept a different gospel from the one you accepted, you submit to it readily enough . . . And what I do I will continue to do, in order to undermine the claim of those who would like to claim that in their boasted mission they work on the same terms as we do. For such men are false apostles, deceitful workmen, disguising themselves as apostles of Christ. And no wonder, for even Satan*

disguises himself as an angel of light. So it is not strange if his servants also disguise themselves as servants of righteousness.

To say that Jesus Christ was the first transcendental meditator is "preaching another Jesus" than the one the apostles preached. It is also teaching a different gospel than the one preached in the Bible. The apostle Paul has commented on similar issues in his first letter to Timothy 1:3-7:

> *. . . that you may charge certain persons not to teach any different doctrine, nor to occupy themselves with myths and endless genealogies which promote speculations rather than the divine training that is in faith; whereas the aim of our charge is love that issues from a pure heart and a good conscience and sincere faith. Certain persons by swerving from these have wandered away into vain discussion, desiring to be teachers of the law, without understanding either what they are saying or the things about which they make assertions.*

And in I Timothy 1:19:

> *By rejecting conscience, certain persons have made shipwreck of their faith . . .*

Within the world of TM® there are many myths which promote speculations. CC, GC, UC and Brahman Consciousness are theoretical descriptions which become all-absorbing foci of the initiators and many meditators. I know that I did not have a clear conscience about deceiving people into believing that TM® is not religious. Obviously, I was not alone, as can be seen by reading the stories of Chris Meade and Gregory Randolph in Appendixes 3 and 4. Yet I did have a desire—based on a rather common mixture of spiritual greed and honest but untested idealism—to be a teacher of a "law" or a "way" to improve the quality of life. For the same reason, many teachers of TM®, lured by the big prize of higher consciousness, simply parrot the words of Maharishi without really understanding what they are saying. I myself at times stated to people that the teaching of TM® is to be found in the Bible. When I finally decided to take a long and serious look at what the Bible really had to say, I was quite surprised to learn that this isn't the case.

Is the TM® movement more in harmony with the light of God or with an angel of light? The indications are strong that the TM® teachings parallel those of the angel of light rather than the inspired teachings of God as recorded in the Bible.

In the Christian Science usage of the word "devil" we found that one of the meanings was "hypnotism." Hypnotism is a technique for heightening a person's suggestibility or opening him to influences other than himself. The TM® movement claims to have physiological evidence that the "restful alertness" experienced during TM® is quite different from that experienced during hypnosis. They base this claim on oxygen consumption and brain wave patterns.

Is this claim justified? I say no. It and many others are in serious question today, as Appendix 5 points out. In addition, *Nova,* the National Educational Television network's weekly science program, had one show in late 1975 that provided still more evidence in the case against the accuracy of much of the TM® research supporting the concept of the physiological uniqueness of the TM® experience.

To those critiques I would add the following: I have instructed in the practice of TM® individuals who had previously practiced self-hypnosis and who experienced very similar subjective states during both TM® and self-hypnosis. There is a belief among some professionals that hypnosis is not in and of itself a physiologically defined state, but rather is a technique for altering one's level of suggestibility. The accompanying physiological changes may differ from individual to individual. It is possible, therefore, that some individuals may have similar experiences during both TM® and any of a number of forms of hypnosis.

109

A former medium, mentioned in Gordon Lewis's book, makes the point for me through his description of the early phases of becoming a medium:

Raphael Gasson, a former medium, explains that in a student's first session he learns to relax his body and to keep his mind on one thing until he has reached a state of what could be regarded as self-hypnosis and passivity, which results in his not thinking for himself. He becomes an automaton through which evil spirits work by taking advantage of his passivity.

Maharishi's promised cosmic consciousness sounds a lot like the above description except that it is on a more permanent basis. Remember that CC is described as a subjective state of a "moment of silence" in the midst of activity, a separation of the self from activity, as if being a "witness of one's self," a sense of "doing less and accomplishing more."

A friend of mine, Andy, who is still an active meditator and initiator, once described an experience he had in a rounding course (residence course) during a period of long meditation. He said he reached a point where he was no longer breathing for himself—he felt he was "being breathed." His interpretation of this experience was that he had merged with the Absolute and had gained a temporary state of CC. From the TM® point of view, Andy had been sitting in a relaxed position thinking a meaningless sound with vibrational qualities which would reduce his mental activity until he achieved mental refinement to the extent that his conscious awareness settled to the source of thought, otherwise known in SCI terminology as the field of pure creative intelligence, or the Absolute (Enlightenment Factory terminology from the early days).

From a Christian point of view, however, Andy was worshipping and calling upon the name of a Hindu (and therefore false) deity. He was opening himself to foreign influences and could very well expect to have an experience of "being breathed" or possessed by some being or creature indigenous to a spiritistic realm.

Theologian William Johnston, a student of mysticism, is also quoted in Lewis:

> *All religious traditions know of a mysticism of evil. I remember being shocked when I first heard of a 'samadhi of pure evil.' Because of a possible bad meditative 'trip' traditional mysticism required an aspiring meditator to have 'undergone a conversion and be totally dedicated to good.' Do the teachers of TM take this precaution?*

Maharishi might reply to the above in terms of unstressing. He would perhaps say that the bad meditative trip is nothing more than a little roughness in the middle of some good unstressing, clearing out too many "crumpled cellophane balls" of stress too quickly and thereby creating some discomfort temporarily. He would then point out that after the experience was over, there would be a greater sense of stability or of being more grounded in that silence within as a result of the removal of another block of stress.

Here is another quote from Lewis's book:

> *As indicated above, one may open himself to the influence of demons. Dr. Elmer Green of the. Menninger Clinic said, "According to various warnings, the persistent explorer in these realms . . . brings himself to the attention of indigenous beings, who under normal circumstances pay little attention to humans . . . They are of many natures and some are malicious, cruel and cunning."*

Is it fair to link this false worship to demonic possession? If there is a link, could such activity lead to demonic possession? My answer is yes; and here's why.

Christians say that false worship results from a lack of understanding about true worship of the living God, our heavenly Father and the Father of Jesus. In other words, misleading teachings such as "becoming like God," etc. (which Satan, in the form of the serpent, gave to Eve) will lead one away from true worship of the Creator into a false worship of idols, creatures and false gods. As we have seen, these teachings come from Satan. But is Satan a demon? Satan is identified as the ruler of the demons in Matthew 12:24-26:

> But when the Pharisees heard it they said, "It is only by Be-el'zebub, the prince of demons, that this man casts out demons." Knowing their thoughts, He [Jesus] said to them, "Every kingdom divided against itself is laid waste, and no city or house divided against itself will stand; and if Satan casts out Satan, he is divided against himself; how then will his kingdom stand?"

The Pharisees were accusing Jesus of using demonic power to cast out demons. Jesus replied to their accusation by identifying Beelzebub as Satan. He pointed out that Satan would be defeating his own purpose by permitting Jesus to cast out demons in the name of the head demon. So Satan is not only a demon—he is the prince of demons.

What are demons? Where do they come from? What is their purpose? We find an explanation in Revelation 12:7-9, 12:

> Now war arose in heaven, Michael and his angels fighting against the dragon; and the dragon and his angels fought, but they were defeated and there was no longer any place for them in heaven. And the great dragon was thrown down, that ancient serpent, who is called the Devil and Satan, the deceiver of the whole world—he was thrown down to the earth, and his angels were thrown down with him . . . Rejoice then, O earth and sea, for the devil has come down to you in great wrath, because he knows that his time is short!

So Satan and his demonic forces are at work in the vicinity of earth. They are "fallen angels" who are no longer in God's favor. Judgment has already been passed on them, and hence their "time is short." We learn in Matthew 25:41 that

Satan's angels will be destroyed with him as well as his unrighteous human servants:

> Then he will say to those at his left hand, "Depart from me, you cursed, into the eternal fire prepared for the devil and his angels . . ."

For this reason—the fact that they know they will be destroyed—they are out to mislead as many people as possible into any available form of false worship. In II Corinthians 4:4 we find,

> In their case the god of this world has blinded the minds of the unbelievers, to keep them from seeing the light of the gospel of the glory of Christ, who is the likeness of God.

Here we see Satan, the prince of demons, a fallen angel, referred to as "the god of this world." If the prince of demons is identified as a god, then worship of a false god could well link false worship to demonic influences.

I have made this long discussion in order to present the purpose of the demons during their remaining short time. Their purpose is to keep as many people as possible from entering into the new age. The devil and his demons would like to bring all humanity with them to their destruction. To that end they do everything they can to mislead people into false worship.

Have we yet seen a link between false worship and demonic possession? No, not yet. But false worship is the result of demonic deception. This activity is prophesied in I Timothy 4:1-2:

> Now the Spirit expressly says that in later times some will depart from the faith by giving heed to deceitful spirits and doctrines of demons, through the pretentions of liars whose consciences are seared.

We now see, however, that to be absorbed in false teachings or false worship is to be under the influence of demons and even the devil himself. This is shown in II Timothy 2:25-26:

God may perhaps grant they will repent and come to know the truth, and they may escape from the snare of the devil, after being captured by him to do his will.

In one sense of the word "possession," then, anyone doing the will of Satan is caught by him, ensnared by him, and is therefore in his possession. This is not, however, the same as bodily possession wherein a demon or a fallen angel or a false god enters the body of a human. Instances described in the Bible, such as Luke 8:27-30, indicate that insanity or madness is one result of this other sort of possession.

Is there any evidence that this kind of possession has taken place as a result of practicing TM®? There is, and we'll now look at the actual experiences of meditators which in my view confirm this statement.

Chapter Nine

UNWELCOME VISITORS:
TM® AND DEMONIC POSSESSION—II

A news story entitled "TM Demons and the Great Crawl for Piety," appearing in the *New Haven Advocate* (23 June 1976), provides yet another voice in support of my contention that TM® is intimately linked with the work of the devil:

> *Evangelist Billy Graham warned recently that people who practice transcendental meditation run the risk of possession by demons. Graham told reporters in San Diego, "The Bible says we are to meditate on God. The Bible says we are to meditate on His word."*
>
> *Graham is seriously upset about the threat of competition from evil quarters. "We need more meditation but meditation in the right direction, because if you just empty your mind, demonic power might come in."*

Billy Graham's analysis of the TM® technique was made on the basis of the TM® promise of transcending the mental activity of thinking to reach the "source of thought" during those moments of no-mantra-and-no-thought. Strangely, there are people within the TM® movement who will

115

interpret the phrase "meditate on His word" as meaning to think the mantra effortlessly. If confronted with the fact that the mantras are not meaningless but are really the names of Hindu deities, a likely reply from the TM® movement might be that by using the mantra we are even "meditating on God." These interpretations of Scriptural admonitions are more twisted than a box of pretzels. I myself was one of those who believed "the Word" was "the mantra."

Since TM® is a technique which seems to actively invoke demonic forces, and if humans do have a natural resistance to such forces (Maharishi teaches that the body naturally resists any foreign deposits or inceptions), then it seems likely that to invite or invoke demonic influences might well activate that natural resistance quite spontaneously.

In January, 1974, my wife and I enjoyed the company of Charlie Lutes over dinner at a small Indian restaurant in New York City. Charlie, you remember, is the director of the Spiritual Regeneration Movement, the original TM® organization founded by Maharishi. Charlie attributes his esoteric wisdom to his long and close association with Maharishi.

As we sat at the table, our conversation turned to the possibility of demonic possession, and Charlie acknowledged that possibility. He said that indicators of attempted possession by a demon are tightness in the shoulders and the neck. He said that this is the natural resistance of the person to the demon's attempted entrance. He was making this point with reference to the use of drugs, but we find an interesting reference to this experience of pressure in the neck under the heading "Symptoms of Incorrect Meditation" in the *Three Days Checking* material used during the three follow-up sessions after the day of initiation into TM®:

> One thing is important—that we don't speak of these unless they come up, but in case they do then we make it clear that these experiences indicate incorrect meditation.

Pressure in forehead or back of head, or pain in the temples or pain in the neck. This means forcing, some effort is creeping into the process . . . the natural flow is hindered; this is due to individual effort. (How to correct it) Stop thinking the mantra—effort has started.

Pain or pressure in the neck indicates that some tendency to concentrate has started. Again we advise him to stop the mantra and roll the head slowly with eyes closed and massage to relieve pressure during 30 seconds while mantra is stopped.

. . . main point is: *not* to persist in repeating the mantra. (Emphasis is Maharishi's.)

It seems possible, then, that since in repeating the mantra we are calling on demonic forces, there is a likelihood that an attempted entry may occur. As we saw in Raphael Gasson's description of how to become a medium, it would be unnoticed if the state of passivity and calm is achieved, which results in one's not thinking for himself. The person then becomes the automaton or medium through which evil spirits may work by taking advantage of the passivity. If one is practicing TM® properly, the result is exactly that state of quiet passivity. Maharishi instructs meditators not to exert any effort into the thinking process.

The medium is obviously taken unaware by the entering spirit. If the medium is not in the correct state of awareness, then the spirit would not be able to work through him as easily. In TM®, then, the result of "exerting individual effort into the thinking process" might be another set of words to describe the natural resistance of the meditator to the attempted entry by the demon. Hence the experience of the pain and pressure in the neck, head and temples. If TM® is a demonic ploy designed to bring people nonconsciously into closer union with demonic forces, then it would most definitely be "incorrect meditation" to be in a state of mind where the natural resistance to possession is able to function. The best way to turn that switch off would be to stop thinking the mantra until the discomfort of the resistance passes. Once the mind is off floating unaware and the person is feeling relaxed and comfortable again, he can begin the invocation of the spirit with the repetition of the mantra.

Long periods of rounding could produce more powerful takeovers or possessions and also stronger resistances to the spiritistic influence. This could well explain the bizarre experiences of "unstressing" at the Estes Park teacher training course. That type of experience—Eric being thrown across the room from his meditative pose; involuntary bodily movements, jerkings; visions of green eyes floating in the room—are common to all teacher training and long rounding courses. Do meditators ever wonder about these experiences? Strangely enough, almost all meditators and active initiators believe wholeheartedly in Maharishi's explanation that all of this is "just unstressing." Some initiators do acknowledge the reality of a spiritistic realm inhabited by demons, but they feel that TM® is, if anything, a suit of armor against any attacks by such creatures, that the presence of Maharishi on the rounding courses adds additional protection, if it is ever needed. The following experience of a young female initiator at my wife's teacher training course in La Antilla, Spain forced me to reevaluate those assumptions.

The girl claimed that during meditation a demonic creature jumped down her throat, temporarily possessing her. She was terrified and refused to meditate again. Apparently she became very difficult to deal with, and the course doctor (who was not an unbiased member of the medical community outside the esoteric world of TM® but in fact one of Maharishi's very close associates) locked her in the clinic (an adobe beach house) and kept her under sedation for many weeks. The whole situation was kept very hush-hush. The treatment she ultimately received from concerned initiators who were aware of the situation was a concentrated program of checking to reestablish her routine of meditation. That took many months, and she was apparently reprogrammed to view her experience as "just some unstressing."

In January, 1973, five months after my wife began to practice TM®, she had an unsettling experience. She was driving to work, traveling at moderate speed, perhaps forty miles per hour, when she felt the car swerve uncontrollably back and forth and then the car was bounced up and down. The road was smooth and the shock absorbers were in good condition, so she didn't understand the reason for the movements. Then on the right front fender of the car she saw a short, squat, ghoulish creature with a high strained forehead and bulging, glaring eyes. It was looking through the windshield directly at her! She was absolutely terrified and looked away. When she looked again, it was gone. She called me from work to tell me about it, but I assured her that everything was all right.

I was not shocked with my wife's sighting of a demonic creature. During my years of association with the TM® movement I had heard many stories of similar unusual sightings. Stuart, a very close friend and initiator, saw a procession of spirits above the puja table every time he performed the ceremony. He described some of these creatures as being orbs of light, occasionally calling them angels.

My wife also began to see the creatures of light floating above the puja table and on other occasions floating through walls, doors, and rooms. Some may dismiss this as mere suggestibility, but on occasion I have witnessed Stuart and my wife both seeing the same procession of spirit creatures simultaneously and without any advance warning or notice being given by one to the other.

During our dinner meeting with Charlie Lutes the following year, my wife described her experience to Charlie, particularly the one with the ghoulish demonic creature on the car. He listened attentively and pulled a picture from his pocket. The subject of the picture was a gargoyle, like the ones found on European churches. Charlie asked her if the creature she had seen was similar to the gargoyle. She said it was almost identical. He said that such demons did exist and thus is was very important never to look into their eyes if she saw one again. He talked about the creatures of light, also giving the same instruction about not staring at them, but he indicated that the angels of light should not be a cause for alarm. He asked her how she felt about them, and she said that both kinds of spirits created an uneasiness within her.

It is interesting to note here that if Stuart, Charlie Lutes, and my wife are not all derailed on the same mental train (which I do not believe to be the case), then there is a strong likelihood that the gargoyles found on buildings throughout the world are not just figments of sculptors' clever imaginations, but they are actual representations of creatures sighted by both artists and common folk in altered states of awareness.

Jealous Angels?

What about the angels which Maharishi talked about at Estes Park? In Chapter 2 I mentioned that, according to Maharishi, a group of angels attended the teacher training course. He made the point that the angels were jealous of humans because they couldn't meditate and therefore couldn't experience the same unification of the relative physical plane and the absolute spiritual plane that we humans could through the practice of TM®. Why had the angels been at the course if they couldn't meditate? I did not question Maharishi's statement that the course had been as valuable for the angels as it had been for us. Of what benefit could it have been for them? According to my current understanding of angelology, there are two markedly different classes of angelic creatures. There are angels of God who serve him joyfully in cooperation with God's human servants, as noted in Revelation 22:8-9:

> *I John am he who heard and saw these things. And when I heard and saw them, I fell down to worship at the feet of the angel who showed them to me; but he said to me, "You must not do that! I am a fellow servant with you and your brethren the prophets,*

and with those who keep the words of this book.
Worship God."

And then there are the fallen angels, who work with Satan in defiance of Good and all worshippers of Him to mislead and deceive the entire inhabited earth.

The angel in Revelation 22:8-9 doesn't seem to be jealous of John. He doesn't say, "John, I sure wish I could practice TM® like you." He says he is a fellow servant of God along with John. So who would be the jealous angels be?

The jealous angels would be the rebellious angels who have been thrown out of heaven and restricted to the vicinity of the earth. Knowing they are about to be destroyed and that all men on earth still have the chance to repent and be included in the promised new kingdom, they would have every possible reason to be jealous. They would feel that they had gained so much from the teacher training course because all of us at the course had been rounding for almost three months and laying ourselves open to their machinations the entire time. We would be useful tools indeed in spreading their false teachings far and wide after we returned to our homes in the towns and cities across the country and around the world. There was a widespread belief among many initiators after the course that each of us had picked up at least one and perhaps two or three "guardian angels" upon becoming initiators. Driving back across the country to Connecticut after the Estes Park course ended, one of my traveling companions commented that he felt such a presence with us. And if, as Maharishi says, they want to be able to experience the same unification of the relative physical plane along with the "absolute spiritual plane," what better way than to use the passive meditators as mediums and take possession of them and experience that "harmony" through them?

Final Thoughts about Demonism

In Chris Meade's article (Appendix 4) there is a report of an incident involving an Israeli woman and her concern about the necessity of bowing before the altar of Guru Dev in order to be an initiator. I was there when that incident took place. I flew there to be with my wife, arriving near the end of April—a few weeks prior to the end of the course. I remember the incident well and would like to add a little more detail to the dialogue that took place between Maharishi and the concerned Jews.

The woman made the point that to bow before an image would be in direct conflict with her religious beliefs, that if she took part in the act she would be sentenced to hell by God. Maharishi was quick to reply, "Well, if we go to hell, at least we all go to hell together!" and he laughed heartily. The majority of the 1,500 course participants present joined in with his laughter. My wife and I felt very uncomfortable. Maharishi seemed to be intentionally making fun of the woman's religious beliefs rather than taking a loving concern in her interests. His comment did not go well with his "sacred trappings"and supposed "holiness."

Another interesting incident: a mother attending the course with her young son told me that the boy had given a flower to Maharishi shortly before, and when he looked up at Maharishi's face, all he saw was a glowing ball of light! The mother thought it beautiful that her son was having such "spiritual experiences."

And another: the Maharishi International University clinic, an adobe beach house at the course, closed on or about Friday, May 11, 1973, one week before my wife's course ended. On Sunday, May 13, 1973, a young girl named Barbara, who was about to receive her mantras from Maharishi to finally become an initiator, arrived at the big blue tent on the beach requesting to see Maharishi. She was acting very strangely, as if possessed. A scene ensued between her and Maharishi's "palace guards," who refused to let her see him. She apparently only wanted help, and she figured Maharishi would be the one to see.

She was taken to the nurse, who had a room in one of the hotels quite a distance from the tent. The nurse, who was not an initiator, but who nevertheless knew how to perform the puja, had Barbara perform the puja, ostensibly to calm her down with the "spiritual influence" from the ceremony. In the middle of the puja the nurse gave Barbara two shots in the neck of Haldol and Benadryl.

She was taken to her room by the nurse and told to stay there and rest. Her room was in the same apartment building as my wife's, three floors above us. I knew Barbara well and was aware that she had a previous history of emotional difficulties which had surfaced one year earlier at the same point during the teacher training course which had been held in Fiuggi Fonte, Italy. For that reason she had not been able to receive her mantras and become an initiator, so she returned the following year to Spain in hopes of attaining her dream of becoming a TM® teacher.

That afternoon my wife and I returned to our apartment to find our door wide open. Barbara was there, standing against the dining table in our combination living-dining room with her back to us. At the time we knew nothing about the incident earlier in the day. So far as we knew, she had been doing very well and was emotionally stable. She had seemed fairly confident that she would have no difficulty completing the course this time. I made a friendly joke as we walked in, saying that we had caught her red-handed stealing some fruit from our table. Then she turned around. Her eyes seemed on fire, yet they were deep black pools, totally lost and confused. Obviously she was not in control of herself, and the only words she spoke were a faint whisper as if from another planet: "Help me."

I was somewhat familiar with mental illness. Perhaps Barbara's condition could better be defined as a "psychotic break" of some sort. Whatever the words used to describe her condition, though, she was not in possession of herself. She was in the possession of "something" which was not life-supporting, whatever it was. Neither my wife nor I felt qualified to care for her properly, so we made her comfortable on the sofa, and I went in search of either the course doctor or one of the two nurses.

During the following two days, my wife and I and

several friends spent most of our time trying to convince the medical staff that Barbara needed medical attention. We tried to reach Jerry Jarvis, the U.S. National Director of the TM® movement, and even Maharishi himself with the news of Barbara's situation. We were always confronted with the same story: "They don't have time to waste on such unimportant matters. They aren't interested in hearing about it." The course clinic had been shut down long before it should have been; the medical personnel were acting incompetently, providing inadequate care for Barbara. So we were left to care for her. There we were, course participants at an international university, forced to act as psychiatrists and doctors. It was criminal.

On the evening of May 15, Barbara began to scream and pound on the wall in her room. Her roommate came to us for help. The only thing the course doctor and nurses had done during the preceding two days was to show up periodically and inject her with more Haldol and Benadryl. It was up to us to bring her food and drink. At about 5 PM I went to the initiators' dining hall to get the doctor. He refused to come. I asked him if he was indeed a true doctor who had taken the Hippocratic oath. He said "Yes" but that he was off duty when he was eating dinner. Two young female initiators sitting on either side of him giggled. In disgust I left the dining hall and returned to Barbara and my wife. Barbara was still having convulsive fits and was occasionally gagging on her own tongue. When I related my encounter with the course doctor to my wife, she immediately jumped up, told me to stay with Barbara, and ran to the initiators' dining hall.

As she approached the doctor, he made a hostile remark about that bothersome pain-in-the-neck initiator who had just left and then asked her if she was going to bug him too. My wife described Barbara's condition and her need for treatment. She stated that she would report the doctor for malpractice and refusal to treat a patient in need if he didn't get up immediately and attend to his patient. His reply was shocking: "If you don't get out of here right now, I'm going to kill you." He said this in all seriousness. There was absolutely no humorous intent in his voice.

If Barbara was not possessed by a demon, I am sure the course doctor was. Here was the official course doctor—such a part of the inner circle that he always sat close to Maharishi during lectures and always hung around with Jerry Jarvis—and yet he refused to treat a suffering fellow human because he was at supper. If a person is judged by the company he keeps, Maharishi and Jerry Jarvis stand damned by the incredible callousness of that man. This incident led my wife and me into extremely serious doubts about wanting to continue our association with the TM® movement.

That night at 9:30, one of the course nurses and a meditating astrologer who spent most of her time giving readings at the clinic said they would be taking Barbara to the clinic. We pointed out that the clinic was closed. One of our friends who was helping to care for Barbara asked the nurse if someone would be staying with her that night. The nurse angrily answered, "No!" Barbara was literally dragged down the street that foggy evening and locked up in the adobe beach house that had earlier been the course clinic on the beach.

During the next few days, Barbara found a way to break out of the house and came to visit us a few times. She said she was feeling a little better, and she did seem to have a bit more control over herself. She returned to the U.S. on the charter flight at the end of the course, and we visited with her upon our return to the States in the middle of June after touring Spain for four weeks. She was still meditating and was still contemplating attending more courses.

During my first course with Maharishi at Poland Springs, a girl "freaked out" and was attended by an initiator whom I came to know a few years later. At Estes Park, when I became an initiator, there were no incidents of this sort, so far as I am aware. However, at Amherst in 1971 a very similar situation developed, except the "casualty" this time was a young man about 28 years old. He began to show

125

symptoms of "tripping" on LSD, wandering around the campus of the University of Massachusetts (the location of the one-month course) in the middle of the night.

I visited him in the locked ward of the nearby state mental hospital. He was strapped down to his bed, and four male attendants were caring for him. Apparently he had gotten extremely violent the night before. I called his parents to notify them about what had happened and asked if I could do anything to help. They were not in agreement with his attending the course in the first place and said that I should just let him work out his own solution. He was in no condition to work out anything; when I returned to the campus I found there was to be no help from the TM® movement either. If I wanted to aid the man, it would be on my own time and with my own money, I was told by Jerry Jarvis. I was in no position to transport the man to his home in Illinois, so I left that course feeling helpless. The condition of the man bore a striking resemblance to Barbara's condition in Spain. He was unable to communicate his wishes to me, as if there were some force keeping him locked up inside himself. The girl who claimed to have seen a demon jump down her throat was in a similar condition a year or two earlier after a course in California. My friend Eric was about to board a plane with her to bring her home to her parents in Connecticut, but the pilot would not permit her on board. She ended up in a mental hospital in California.

While I was working late one night at the Institute of Living, a phone call came in from a young man, an initiator, in the Midwest—Kansas, as I recall. I spoke to him for more than half an hour. He told me that ever since he had become an initiator in Spain, he had been experiencing severe emotional problems. The reason he called the Institute was because he knew we were doing research on TM® and he thought perhaps we would be aware of any specialized emotional problems relating to TM®. He wanted help badly because he said he had a strong desire to kill both his parents that evening. I urged him to contact the local mental health center immediately and then talked until he felt he had things under control.

Chris Meade described a pervasive uneasiness after his teacher training course. As mentioned in Chapter 8, and as we see from these other stories, his experience was mild and far from unique.

These experiences, particularly the man in Amherst and Barbara in Spain, sound frighteningly similar to the demon possession described in Luke 8:27-30:

> *And as he stepped out on land, there met him a man from the city who had demons; for a long time he had worn no clothes, and he lived not in a house but among the tombs . . . (For many a time it—the unclean spirit—had seized him; he was kept under guard, and bound with chains and fetters, but he broke the bonds and was driven by the demon into the desert.) Jesus then asked him, "What is your name?" And he said, "Legion"; for many demons had entered him.*

Since I have not yet met anyone who claimed to be in CC and since Maharishi hints that a few people "pop into CC" at every large course but that they would remain anonymous, and since the experience of a medium is markedly similar to the TM® experience, perhaps, as I suggested earlier, if CC is another term for demon possession, then I have indeed met many of those "lucky" few who gain that "separation of self from activity." That separation is not a pretty sight to behold from the outside, and I do not believe that any of the aforementioned TM® casualties were experiencing anything even close to what might be called bliss. In every instance when I was with those people or speaking with them on the phone, they were terrified because they felt completely out of control of what was happening to them.

Conclusion

If one is already on the broad road leading to

damnation, it would make sense for Satan to support any actions and desires of that person. Since Satan is the "god of this world," and if a person did not believe either in him or the one true God of Christianity, then that person would readily interpret any material, physical, emotional, and psychological blessings of the devil as being a non-religious "support of nature." This is precisely how the TM® movement describes the first few years' experience of the "measured" progressive improvement of an individual who begins the practice of TM®.

The life of a Christian is indeed a joyous one filled with great love, a clean conscience and numerous other blessings. However, the Bible says in II Timothy 3:12-13,

> *Indeed all who desire to live a godly life in Christ Jesus will be persecuted, while evil men and imposters will go on from bad to worse, deceiver and deceived.*

And in John 15:20-21, we find Jesus speaking to his disciples:

> *Remember the word that I said to you, "A servant is not greater than his master." If they persecute me, they will persecute you; if they kept my word they will keep yours also. But all this they will do to you on my account, because they do not know him who sent me.*

Likewise in I Peter 3:14:

> *But even if you do suffer for righteousness' sake you will be blessed.*

So the TM® movement's teachings will not lead one to being found spotless and without blemish in the eyes of God. Relaxation and feeling good are not prerequisites to being a good Christian. I am not saying that it is wrong to relax or feel good. These should not, however, become gods themselves. The ultimate good is God, not TM®.

Is TM® a road leading to demonic possession? Maharishi's explanation of the TM® experience in terms of progressive refinement of the nervous system through stress release does not adequately explain the existence of the deceitful practices, lack of human concern, negative social behavior, spiritual greed, spiritual pride, dishonesty and other negative traits found among long-time TM® practitioners who should be displaying quite the opposite qualities if they are indeed growing in true spirituality.

My reason and experience have led me to conclude that TM® stems from the teachings of the angel of light and is therefore part of a vast plan for demonic deception leading to demonic possession. I feel that this explanation of the TM® experience provides a more solid rationale for the lack of positive qualities in the long-time meditators and for the deceitful and dishonest practices of the TM® movement than does Maharishi's pseudoscientific explanation, and I offer it for your consideration.

But in the end, faith is the missing ingredient which is required to complete either of these theories, and that ingredient can only be supplied by each of us individually.

Chapter Ten

CONSCIENCE VS. TM®:
Why I Left the Movement

Two letters I received recently from friends who are still deeply absorbed in the world of TM® express similar sentiments. One from a teacher who attended the same teacher training course as I did in 1970 reads, ". . . but I think it's tragic that you, who were so 'on the track,' should choose to betray and oppose Maharishi for your own personal reasons and advantage." And from a friend who learned TM® in the course that I taught back in 1971, and who has since gone on to become a TM® teacher, comes this statement: "It's very difficult for me to understand why and how you can say the things you do about the TM® program when they run so exactly opposite to my own experience with it."

Because I still have warm regard for these people and try—as the apostle Paul urged—to hate the sin but love the sinner, I feel I should reply publicly. So I will explain the development of my feelings which led, first, to my decision to stop teaching TM®; second, to my discontinuation of the practice of TM® a few months later; and last of all, why more than two years later I felt that a book about the situation was in order.

My transition from inside TM® to outside TM® was not a simple matter. It was not a quick decision, nor was it the result of just one unpleasant experience. Amid the confusion and the mixed emotions I was feeling, the overriding mood was sadness and disappointment. For six years I had practiced TM®. For four of those years TM® was my entire life. During those years I never had any real indications that my feelings would change. Until the spring of 1973 there was never a doubt in my mind that TM® could solve every problem facing the world today—if not directly, then indirectly.

There were, however, numerous experiences, prior to the spring of 1973, which would have led me to doubt the validity of many TM® claims had I been in a reasonable frame of mind. But I wasn't. I readily interpreted any inconsistencies between what was being promised and what was actually happening within the movement as "unstressing" or "normalization" at either my individual level or perhaps on the more "cosmic" level of the TM® movement itself. Those inconsistencies or weaknesses within the movement were, I told myself, simply manifestations of the necessary growth pains resulting from rapid development on the way to becoming a perfect organization. Or perhaps my own speedy development was creating similar growth pains within me which affected my perceptions to the extent that I was incapable of honestly evaluating anything, particularly those obviously negative traits of the movement and many of its members. The net effect was this: I marched along and pretended there were no problems, even though the appearances were quite the opposite. Why? Because I had swallowed the party line that "if you just keep meditating, it won't be long before cosmic consciousness embraces you and that state of awareness beyond morality, beyond the relative values of good and evil, will free you from the petty concerns of this crude, temporal, gross existence."

In so many words that is the meaning of the often-heard statements, "Oh, come on, don't worry about *that*—you're just unstressing. Ignore the problem, do nothing about it now. Just keep meditating— and throw all your trust and faith on Maharishi. Things will improve." That was my attitude.

It is this same attitude which provides the movement leaders with a perfect excuse to disregard numerous organizational problems. And by the same token it provides individuals, movement leaders, initiators and meditators alike the opportunity to ignore any negative personal traits within themselves and sweep them under the rug.

One promise, for example, is that model societies will result from everyone practicing TM®. As Chris Meade so clearly describes in Appendix 4, at the teacher training course which he and my wife attended, and which I spent three weeks observing in April, 1973, it was all too clear that the norm of the course was disorganization, ineptness, clumsy bureaucracy, poor communication, indifference of movement personnel to these problems, and poor and overcrowded accommodations. In addition, it was at this course that many of the unpleasant experiences which are described in Chapters 8 and 9 took place. Keep in mind that this course was not unique. These conditions to one degree or another were common to every TM® course I attended, and to many which I didn't attend but heard described. Yet these courses were planned and executed by those who, according to the movement, would be the leaders of a "model meditating society."

Maharishi is currently holding six-month training courses in Switzerland, at a cost of $4,000 per person, to produce "Governors" of the "Age of Enlightenment." I have never heard of a form of government which "produces" governors for a fee. Apparently Maharishi has political ideas and plans for world rule. Appendix 6 deals with the political and spiritual implications of the attitude implicit in the existence of a course such as Maharishi is currently teaching. I find them frightening.

The government which would lead the "Age of Enlightenment" as described by Maharishi would, of necessity, require that everyone practice TM®. I have heard Maharishi say on occasion that in the society he envisions, if someone is not smiling or happy he would be picked up by a meditation paddy wagon and taken to a checking facility for the proper TM® treatment and then released. That is not the kind of society I wish to live in.

But to return. There were numerous inconsistencies of this sort—some of which I have described earlier—which should have raised doubts in me but didn't because of my blinding, zealous idealism and my desire to believe in the goodness of TM® and Maharishi. This attitude epitomizes the majority of the proponents of the TM® movement. As a result, it would have been well nigh impossible for me, four years ago, to understand why I feel the way I do today. So I don't really expect many TM® teachers to fully understand or appreciate the reasons for the change in my beliefs and feelings. I wish it were otherwise. I can only present the facts as I see them and hope that, at the very least, they will be recognized as facts. I expect that many more TM® meditators who are not teachers will find it somewhat easier to appreciate the reasons.

It is true that many meditators practice TM® religiously. But in general, meditators are not quite so dependent on TM® as teachers are. TM® provides the mainstay of the TM® teacher's life, world view, and in many cases, his livelihood.

In a sense, teaching TM® can be compared realistically to a drug habit. In order to get higher, it is necessary to turn more and more people on to the experience. This aspect of spiritual greed was discussed in Chapter 6. In addition to the "spiritual" rewards gained from teaching TM®, the initiators also receive financial reward in the form of a commission for each person initiated. As a result, the motives for teaching a TM® course from week to week may vary, depending on the financial needs of the initiators. Head counting at introductory lectures in order to estimate the potential income from a course is not uncommon. A fixed amount of money is also set aside for the initiators for each person initiated in the name of ATR (Advanced Training Resource) credits. When a specified number of initiations have been performed by the initiator, he is eligible to attend a rest-and-rounding course free of charge (it is paid for by the financial credits received from each initiation). When I was teaching, one hundred initiations were required. In this way a teacher supports his "enlightenment habit." When he is not "rushing on to enlightenment" at a rest-and-rounding course, he is energetically pushing TM®.

This total involvement in TM® was my experience, and it is one of the reasons why I spent a very difficult year after I faced the truth about TM®. I was forced to totally reevaluate myself—my values, my beliefs and my goals.

As mentioned in Chapter 6, my first awareness of the dark side of TM® was at the post-SCI symposium party in March of 1973. At the party I overheard a somewhat shocking conversation between two TM® teachers whom I knew very well. That incident was followed a month later by a series of events at my wife's teacher training course on the southern coast of Spain which added insult to my already injured respect for the TM® movement. I began to nurture doubts about whether the apparent organizational problems of the TM® movement might be symptomatic of a deeper problem—the TM® technique itself.

Spain

Sue and I were married December 20, 1972. We had agreed that since I was a TM® teacher, it would be best for our marriage if she became a teacher also as soon as possible. As a result, upon completion of her first phase of teacher training in early March, 1973, she made plans to attend the final phase of teacher training, which was to begin less than two weeks later in a small off-season resort town on the southern coast of Spain. Neither of us liked the idea of being separated for three months. However, there seemed to be no other way for Sue to become a teacher, and for the moment our priorities were strongly TM®-oriented.

Within two days of her departure, I felt I probably would not survive three months without even so much as talking to Sue. I missed my wife desperately, and I realized at that point that TM® was not the be-all and end-all of existence. Our marriage had suddenly replaced TM® as my most important concern. Before she left, it had seemed to me that the three-month separation would be worthwhile because Sue would be able to teach TM® with me. However, after just two days of separation, I could think of nothing except how much I missed Sue. Whether she was a teacher or not made no difference.

I immediately began to conclude my studying and teaching activities in order to fly over as soon as possible and be with Sue for the last half of her course. I was finally able to get away at the end of April. I had arranged with movement headquarters to use my ATR credits to pay for my accomodations and meals during my six-week stay, which was to last from the end of April to the first week of June. I had been assured that the course office in Spain would be notified of my coming.

I left New York on an evening flight. We arrived in Madrid next morning, had a five-hour layover and then took off for Seville. An hour after landing there I boarded a bus bound for Huelva, the nearest city to the course location. Another short bus ride and a taxi ride brought me to the front door of a white adobe four-story apartment building. I was exhausted after traveling for almost 24 hours. It had been only six weeks since Sue had left, but it seemed like years.

After a joyful reunion with Sue, I checked in at the housing office to announce my arrival. Imagine my surprise when I was informed that they had received no word from the States about my coming. The fact that a message didn't reach the course office in Spain really didn't disturb me. What did disturb me was the attitude with which they dealt with my problem. I was told they would check with the California office to confirm my story, but that even if it turned out that my ATR credits were applicable to the room and board fees, I should plan on staying at an alternate course location some thirty miles from my wife. Remaining with my wife was strongly discouraged.

I could have understood their point if my wife had female roommates. But from the day she arrived, she had been sharing the apartment with male roommates! The housing office was so disorganized that it had not been able to find adequate accommodations for some of the course participants until well into the third week of the course. One of the would-be teachers slept on the living room floor of the apartment for over a week waiting for another room to open up.

I finally squared things away and moved in with my wife. The room was sparsely furnished with one straight-backed wooden chair, two metal cots and a small porcelain-topped table. The room measured no more than ten feet by ten feet and had a tile floor. One tiny window looked out on more apartment buildings. Together my wife and I were paying a little more than $20 a day for the room and our meals. The meals were not expensive, for the most part consisting of locally grown produce, fish and fowl. Other meat was not included as part of the course menu. In short, expenses for the operation of the course were minimal. Chris Meade discusses this point in his article, so I won't dwell on it except to mention this: immediately after the course ended, my wife and I stayed on in La Antilla with some friends in a small beach cottage. The rental charge for the entire cottage, which included two bedrooms, a bathroom, a kitchen, and a living room, was five dollars a month! We both had our suspicions about what happened to all the money we had spent on the course.

So in addition to my doubts about the spiritual value of the TM® movement, doubts about its financial integrity began gnawing at me. By the end of the course all my doubts had been amply nourished. The callous attitude shown by the course medical staff to the young woman who experienced the severe breakdown (or possession), Maharishi's callous reply to the Jewish woman who expressed concern about TM® conflicting with her religion, plus many other experiences described in earlier chapters left Sue and me feeling confused about the TM® movement.

We toured Spain for four weeks and returned to the U.S. Sue had successfully completed the course and was now an initiator, a full-fledged teacher of TM®. We were both meditating regularly, and we both enjoyed the relaxation which the technique produced. We continued working on our relationship with the organizational side of TM® during July and August. We traveled to Illinois and visited with my folks for a couple of weeks, after which we spent four weeks camping and visiting with a friend who had become an initiator with me back in 1970 and who had also been at the La Antilla course for a period of rest and rounding (ATR course).

While we were camping near Kirkland Lake, Ontario, we had occasion to give an introductory TM® lecture one evening at a local college. The lecture seemed to be going well. We were presenting the usual benefit package in standard movement fashion until suddenly a woman in the back row jumped up and accused us of working for the devil! She said that if TM® really was the marvelous universal cure-all we were promising, then it must be a gift of God and that we obviously must be working for the devil if we were charging money for a gift from God. She and two or three of her friends got up and walked out of the hall. She made a strong impression, but still we brushed her accusation off to the tune of "Poor stressed out ignorant lady; if only she could see how confused she is." On two other occasions during my TM® teaching career I had been cautioned that I was not on the Christian track and to beware.

After returning to Connecticut in late August, we decided to open a small TM® center and lead a busy yet quiet life teaching TM® to the residents of suburbs around Hartford. With the help of loaned money we purchased a large, well-kept Victorian-style home and invited a few other TM® teachers to move in with us to help run the center. Everything seemed to be going well—until October. A friend of ours who was a TM® teacher suggested that we pay a visit to a world-renowned psychic astrologer in New York City. Neither Sue nor I had ever been much interested in astrology. I particularly had been living such a TM® party line life that I had almost intentionally avoided any contact with it, although I was aware that quite a few other TM® teachers were very actively interested in the occult sciences. As it turned out, the majority of this astrologer's clients were TM® teachers. We did pay him a visit, and in addition to finding the reading very interesting, we felt even more that we had found a new friend. He took a strong liking to us also, and so we invited him to spend a weekend with us if he had the chance. He liked the idea very much and took us up on the offer. TM® teachers and meditators from all over the area wanted to come to see him since it was more convenient than traveling to New York. The result of our association with our astrologer friend was a phone call from the East Coast Regional Co-ordinator of the TM® movement in Boston, telling us either to close ourselves down as a TM® center or break off our relationship with the astrologer.

This confrontation sharpened my appreciation for the two-faced nature of the TM® movement. Behind closed doors the TM® movement abounds with esoterica, and many of the teachers are deeply absorbed in occult activities, but in public the movement loudly declares that TM® is as straight as the day is long in midsummer.

Shortly afterward we were visited by friends of Sue who had been studying the Bible. They were not pushy, but they did mention that idolatry and Christianity were opposed to one another, and it seemed that parts of TM® contained strong elements of idol worship. For the first time I began to worry about whether I should continue teaching TM®. During that discussion I tried to explain to Dave (my wife's girlfriend's husband) that learning about the Bible wouldn't make any significant impact on living unless the state of cosmic consciousness was achieved first. I emphasized the importance of the level of consciousness with relation to gaining enlightenment and gaining God's favor. The usual reaction of people upon hearing the TM® level-of-consciousness-is-most-important pitch is either to be in awe, to be confused, or to respond with some equally quasi-philosophical retort in agreement with the TM® view. Dave's reply left me with no comeback. He said that he couldn't care less about cosmic consciousness, that it didn't impress him, that as far as he could see Jesus never seemed one bit concerned about what level of consciousness His followers were in, and that what seemed important to him was honesty, truth and whether or not there was a real concern to follow God's rules as taught in the Bible.

During the next few weeks my mind played through the previous years of association with TM®, and I began to see only too clearly that the rule seemed to be the deception of the public, the dishonesty, the arrogance, the spiritual greed and the spiritual pride of the movement leaders and initiators. I was no longer able to blame the lack of organization or the immaturity of many zealous young teachers on the failings and inconsistencies I had witnessed within the movement.

With my fourth technique in mind I knew that TM® was far from secular, and yet I was still proclaiming in public lectures that TM® was not religious.

At this point the first clear and obvious entrance of conscience took place in my life. I realized that it was not my right to decide for other people what was best for them. Rather, as a teacher my responsibility should be to provide people with all the facts I had at my disposal and then allow them to decide for themselves—with *all* the facts in hand—whether or not to learn TM®.

The transition from that initial realization to the point of actually quitting TM® was not easy. During the years from 1968 to 1973, as I grew increasingly attached to the TM® movement's world view, I sincerely believed that TM® was the "real thing." I did not *want* to arrive at the emotional-philosophical take-off field from the land of TM®. It was never my desire to have conflicts with my conscience over whether TM® was good or evil.

I was quite content with my limited understandings and concepts of life as offered by the TM® movement. At the time, however, I never felt they were limited. How could beliefs which contained the words "absolute," "infinite" and "unbounded" be limited? I now see that beliefs of such a nature can be thoroughly absorbing and can infect your world view to the extent that you envision yourself to be a lighthouse of world-saving wisdom. This is exactly the self-image which the TM® movement instills in its teachers. It sets up a divisive hierarchy between the initiators and everyone they meet. In many cases the point is reached where the initiator denies himself the company of potentially good friends simply because the other person is not also an initiator.

As I see it now, to consider yourself to be the holder of "privileged information" or "secrets of the universe" which must be spoon-fed to the "ignorant majority" of mankind in order not to "confuse" them with the facts, "at least until they're ready," truly limits the scope of your life and your vision. And that "state of readiness" is of course determined by you—not by the person himself.

When all the pieces came together, I decided to quit teaching TM® altogether. The next question which demanded an answer was, "If the TM® movement contains so many immoral and amoral traits, could it then be that the technique itself is the cause of them?"

This question is fully answered under the headings, "The Mystical Roots of Deception" and "Beyond Good and Evil" in Appendix 6. In a few words, however, the goal of TM®, according to Maharishi, is the state of mind which will justify any action, a state of mind beyond morality. In other words, an amoral state of mind. So, based on my analysis of the actions of the TM® movement, I must conclude that TM® does indeed produce the promised result. Any and all actions which may overstep the bounds of conscience are justified or rationalized in the name of "higher consciousness."

Once I realized this connection between what TM® really promised and the fruits of practicing TM®, the decision to quit meditating followed quickly. Although at the time I had no plans to become involved in any other form of worship. I did decide that I definitely was not interested in continuing with my use of the mantra, which I knew to be a devotional practice. Sue and I tried sitting down twice a day to simply close our eyes and rest. However, we found that we couldn't close our eyes without thinking the mantra, so we decided not to do it at all until enough deconditioning had naturally occurred to overcome that automation.

For a time I found myself missing the routine of meditating, but I eventually adjusted to the non-meditating routine. I was pleasantly surprised to find that I actually felt more at ease with myself after I quit than when I had been meditating, even though there were times when I had urges to return to the practice. It would be unreasonable to expect that quitting would be smooth and easy. It had been six years since I began the practice, and during the last four years I had been meditating at least twice a day—and frequently more when I was attending the ATR courses or running checking meetings. Psychologically and physiologically, I was conditioned to a regular routine of meditating.

Changes in living circumstances followed. We closed the house as a TM® center, and the teachers who had been living with us moved out. We were expecting our first child in November. It was then late spring of 1974, and we converted the house to a two-family dwelling in order to make the mortgage affordable. I went to work on a full-time basis as a travel agent. In November, after our first son was born, I attempted a job change which didn't work out, and I then spent a number of months out of work. Finally I began a new job close to home with a company that builds industrial exhibits.

Through the years I had kept in close touch with my friend Willy, informing him about my conflicts with TM®.

He called one day to ask if I had read the recent article in *Time* magazine about a suit which was attempting to block TM® from being taught in the New Jersey public school systems. Willy sent me a copy of the article which, in summary, said that $40,000 of federal tax money had been granted to certain New Jersey public school systems to support the teaching of the Science of Creative Intelligence in the school there. SCI is, of course, just a grandiose name for Transcendental Meditation. Some concerned parents and organizations were filing suit against the TM® movement and certain government agencies, claiming that SCI is nothing more than subtly disguised Hinduism and as such should play no part in public school curricula, let alone be funded by federal tax money. The problem I could see they were going to run into was that unless someone who knew the full truth about TM® was willing to talk, the suit might be lost due to lack of evidence about the religious nature of TM®.

I now realized how far-reaching the effects of the TM® cover-up had spread, and so I decided to give a statement on behalf of the plaintiffs based on my personal experience with TM®. I contacted the plaintiffs' lawyer and met with him to discuss what had been accomplished to date. I was pleasantly surprised to learn that there were other disenchanted ex-TM® teachers who had already come forward and offered statements to the court. Appendix 3 by Gregory Randolph contains one such statement.

After giving my statement, it was suggested that this information could be of value to all who were currently practicing TM®, particularly to all who were yet to consider learning it. Before I could take the step to actually write this book, I had to decide whether it was right for me to break the promise made to my TM® teacher back in 1968 and the promise made to Maharishi in 1970. The question ultimately reduced itself to this: were either of the promises binding? My initiator had asked that I never tell what happened behind closed doors. But she also lied to me about the nature of the ceremony and the supposedly meaningless mantra. Her request for a promise from me was not made in good faith. The contract, I decided, was invalid. Likewise I decided that the same held true for the "Pledge of Loyalty" made upon becoming an initiator. This contract and pledge called for me to mislead the public into believing that TM® was secular in every way. The pledge is also written to give the impression that the tradition to which I bound myself is ancient. As I showed in Chapter 3, the tradition either never existed as such or else was seriously tampered with by Maharishi. So again, I had been lied to.

Conscience, then, led me to conclude that it would be wrong to continue concealing the truth. Conscience also urged me to tell the full story of TM® and to break the pledge which, as I saw it, was never a good-faith pledge to begin with.

The statement I gave to the court provided the basis for writing this book. The positive reactions of friends, meditators, and even a few inactive teachers of TM® encouraged me to continue with the project. I now offer it in the spirit of truth for your consideration.

Appendix 1

The Initiator's Pledge of Loyalty

Upon completion of the TM® teacher training course, an initiator is required to sign the following document.

— — — — — — — —

TO HIS HOLINESS MAHARISHI MAHESH YOGI

It is my privilege, Maharishi, to promise to teach the Principles and Practice of Transcendental Meditation only as a teacher-employee of _____* which accepts me as such; that I will always hold the teaching in trust for you, dear Maharishi, and _____; that I will never use the teaching except as a teacher in _____ or other organisations founded by you for the purpose of carrying on your work of spreading Transcendental Meditation for the good of Mankind; that as a teacher in _____ I shall receive such compensation as shall be agreed between myself and _____ in writing and, except as agreed in writing I expect to receive no monetary compensation but am fully compensated by the love and joy that I receive from the work, by the alleviation of suffering that I may accomplish, and by the Wisdom that I obtain, expound, and cherish. In furtherance of this pledge I acknowledge that

145

prior to receiving the training I had no prior knowledge of such system of Teaching; that there is no other available source where the knowledge of such teaching may be obtained; that such teaching has been imparted to me in trust and confidence; that such training is secret and unique. I further recognise that as a Meditation Guide and Initiator I am a link in the chain of organisations that you have founded; and that to retain the purity of the teaching and movement, you have laid down the wise rule that, should I ever cease to teach in _____ or other organisations founded by you for the purpose of teaching Transcendental Meditation, I may be restrained by appropriate process from using this secret Teaching of Transcendental Meditation imparted to me.

It is my fortune, Guru Dev, that I have been accepted to serve the Holy Tradition and spread the Light of God to all those who need it. It is my joy to undertake the responsibility of representing the Holy Tradition in all its purity as it has been given to me by Maharishi and I promise on your altar, Guru Dev, that with all my heart and mind I will always work within the framework of the Organisations founded by Maharishi. And to you, Maharishi, I promise that as a Meditation Guide I will be faithful in all ways to the trust that you have placed in me.

Jai Guru Dev

DATED: _____   _____

MAHARISHI MAHESH YOGI

_____

_____

INITIATOR

*[The blanks are to be filled in with the name of one of the five organizations which constitute the worldwide TM® movement. R. S.]

146

Appendix 2

The Complete Text of *The Holy Tradition* (Initiator's Manual)

JAI GURU DEV

INTRODUCTION TO THE HOLY TRADITION

The Holy Tradition of the custodians of the eternal wisdom of the integration of life stands as the basis of revivals of understanding about life, which arise from time to time to set man right on the speedy path of evolution, to save him from suffering and to awaken him to live a meaningful life. The Masters of the Holy Tradition have been the exponents of truth, time after time, from times immemorial, they spoke eternal truths of practical life and laid out such standards of living which would guide man to successful life in fulfillment generation after generation.

The teachers of Transcendental Meditation around the world stem from this eternal and universal tradition of great Masters. All the teaching is carried out in the name of these great Masters and on their behalf, and this links every teacher in every generation with the precious line of Masters. This link of the present teacher with the Masters of antiquity is so precious in the life of the teacher that a set system of expressing our gratitude to the Masters has arisen, to maintain the purity and preserve the vitality of the teaching.

The details of the procedure for invoking the Holy Tradition are so perfected that the whole personality of the teacher, his being, his mind, his heart, his body, his atmosphere become one-pointedly directed upon the dignity and the greatness of these great Masters and thus having become saturated in the essence of the Divine wisdom the teacher commences the teaching.

The purpose of the Invocation is to tune our active mind, through the memory of the great Masters to the goal of their wisdom, the Absolute, and from there pick up the mantra and give it to the new initiate; and through that lead his consciousness to the Absolute.

This means that the Initiator takes his awareness or consciousness to the Absolute Being, brings his awareness to the relative, leads the awareness of the initiate from the relative to the Absolute and trains him to incorporate more and more of the Absolute in his relative life.

How does the process of the Invocation help our awareness to reach the Absolute in an active manner? It is the experience of meditators that whenever there is an occasion of silence the awareness starts sinking into deeper levels of the silence. It is not enough for the initiator to let his awareness get to the Absolute. What is necessary is that while his awareness is sinking into silence, his intellect should be awake and he should be able to operate from deep levels of silence.

The traditional process of Invocation is such that automatically the mind reaches the required depth and picks up the mantra to be given to the one seeking initiation. The mechanics by which the process of Invocation succeeds in bringing the initiator's awareness to the depth of thought lies basically in his ability to pronounce the words of the Invocation, and also perform the necessary movements for offerings—as simultaneously the mind dwells on the meaning of the spoken word. This innocent harmony of thought, speech and action certainly increases with practice. As it increases it induces greater ability of sinking deeper into silence while maintaining speech and action.

This increasing ability of maintaining deeper awareness and at the same time, speech and action on the surface, is a direct path to the development of Cosmic Consciousness. This is how, when the initiator is leading the new initiate into Transcendental Consciousness, he himself is rising to Cosmic Consciousness. This explains why and how the initiator feels more and more surcharged with increasing degree of Cosmic Consciousness. That means more energy, more intelligence, more happiness, more freedom from bondage, more liberation, and more fulfillment.

The performance of the Invocation starts with a resolution. This lays open to the intellect the clear possibility of fulfillment of life lived in Supreme Knowledge, in which the Divine Unity becomes a living reality. The situation is that life as it is, is a composite of two spheres — relative and Absolute. The relative is changing and the Absolute is non-changing. Therefore the Absolute is said to be pure and the relative impure. This then presents to us three spheres — relative, Absolute, and the Absolute in the relative. It is present in the waking state of consciousness, the state of pure consciousness and in Cosmic Consciousness. Whatever be the state of life, it is necessary to have life in the celestial field,* or to have activity in the celestial light for Unity to develop and become a living reality.

As the resolution is pronounced and as the hands sprinkle the water, the mind conceives the whole of the outer world and the Inner Being and the continuity of the Inner Being in the outer world. The silent calm water is scattered as drops in the atmosphere, and with that the mind, established in the meaning, dwells on Being manifesting life in all creation. The continuity of inner and outer life is conceived between the calm and the activity. It is a very pleasing and elevating feeling — between the two movements of the hand (or between the state of silence and starting) on the physical and mental planes.

*God Consciousness is the basis to Supreme Knowledge.

The making of the offerings enriches the active atmosphere with the bliss of silence and enlivens the quietness of the area into sublime and blissful activity. The air is automatically sanctified. A calm wave of spiritual influence is generated to produce ethical and mental influences of purification described in the opening words of the Invocation. Having produced this purifying influence in the atmosphere, now is the suitable time to inspire the waves of love and gratitude towards further glorification of the heart and mind. This is spontaneously brought about by the innocent recitation of the names of the Great Masters of the Holy Tradition.

* * * * * * * * *

INVOCATION OF THE HOLY TRADITION

Apavitrah pavitro wa Sarwa wasthan gatopi wa
Yahamaret Pundari-kaksham Sa bahya-abhyantarah
    schuchih

Avahanam

Narayanam Padma-bhawam Vashistham
Shaktim cha tat putra parasharam cha
Vyasam Shukam Gauda-padam mahantam
Govinda Yogindra-mathasya Shishyam
Shri Shankaracharya mathasya Padma-
Padam cha Hasta-malakam cha shishyam
Tam Trotakam Vartik-ka-ramanyan
Asmad gurun santata-manatosmi

Shruti Smriti Purana-nam
Alayam karuna-layam
Namami Bhagawat Padam
Shankaram loka Shankaram
Shankaram Shankaracharyam
Keshawam Badarayanam

150

Sutra bhasya kritau vande
Bhagawantau punah punah
Yad-dware nikhila nilimpa parishad
Siddhim vidhatte-nisham
Shrimat shri lasitam Jagat Gurupadam
Natwatma triptim gatah
Loka-gyana payoda patanadhuram
Shri Shankaram Sharmadam
Brahmananda Saraswatim Guruvaram
Dhya-ya-mi jyotir mayam

Avahanam samarpayami Shri Guru charan kamalebhyo
    namah
Asanam (seat) samarpayami Shri Guru charan kamalebhyo
    namah
Snanam (water) samarpayami Shri Guru charan
    kamalebhyo namah
Vastram (cloth) samarpayami Shri Guru charan
    kamalebhyo namah
Chandanam (sandalpaste) samarpayami Shri Guru charan
    kamalebhyo namah
Akshataan (rice) samarpayami Shri Guru charan
    kamalebhyo namah
Pushpam (flower) samarpayami Shri Guru charan
    kamalebhyo namah
Dhupam (incense) samarpayami Shri Guru charan
    kamalebhyo namah
Deepam (flame) samarpayami Shri Guru charan
    kamalebhyo namah
Achmaniyam (water) samarpayami Shri Guru charan
    kamalebhyo namah
Naivedyam (fruits) samarpayami Shri Guru charan
    kamalebhyo namah
Achmaniyam (water) samarpayami Shri Guru charan
    kamalebhyo namah
Tambulam (betel) samarpayami Shri Guru charan
    kamalebhyo namah
Shri phalam (coconut) samarpayami Shri Guru charan
    kamalebhyo namah

Arartikyam (camphor flame)

Karpura-gauram karuna-vataram Samsara-saram bhuja-
    gendra haram
Sada vasantam hridayara-vinde Bhawam bhawani sahitam
    namami
Arartikyam samarpayami Shri Guru charan
    kamalebhyo namah
Achmaniyam samarpayami Shri Guru charan
    kamalebhyo namah

Pushpanjalim

Gurur Brahma Gurur Vishnur
Gurur Devo Maheshwarah
Guruh Sak-shat Param Brahma
Tasmai Shri Gurave namah
Akhanda mandalakaram
Vyaptam yena characharam
Tat padam darshitam yena
Tasmai Shri Gurave namah
Shri Brahmanandam paramsukhdam
Kevalam gyanmurtim
Vishwateetam gagana sadrisham
Tatwa-masya-di lakshyam
Ekam Nityam Vimalamachalam
Sarvadhi saakshi bhutam
Bhawa-teetam triguna sahitam
Sad-gurum tam namami
Agyana timirandhasya
Gyananjana shalakaya
Chakshu runmilitam yena
Tasmai Shri Gurave namah

Pushpanjalim samarpayami Shri Guru charan
    kamalebhyo namah

****

INVOCATION OF THE HOLY TRADITION

Whether pure or impure, or whether full of purities or
impurities,
Whosoever remembers the lotus-eyed Lord gains inner and
outer purity.

INVOCATION

To Lord Narayan, to lotus-born Brahma the Creator,
to Vaishistha, to Shakti and his son Parashar,
To Vyasa, to Shukadeva, to the great Gaudapada, to
Govinda, ruler among the yogis, to his disciple
Shri Shankaracharya, to his disciples Padma-Padam,
Hasta-Malakam,
To him, Trotakacharya, to Vartik-kar, to others, to the
Tradition of our Masters, I bow down.

To the abode of the wisdom of the Shrutis, Smritis and
Puranas, to the abode of kindness, to the feet of the
Lord Shankaracharya, to the emancipator of the world,
I bow down.

To Shankaracharya the emancipator, hailed as Krishna and
Badarayana, to the commentator of the Brahma Sutras,
I bow down, to the Lord I bow down again and again.

At whose door the whole galaxy of gods pray for perfection
day and night,
Adorned by immeasurable glory, preceptor of the whole
world, having bowed down to Him, we gain fulfillment.
Skilled in dispelling the cloud of ignorance of the people,
the gentle emancipator, Bahmananda Saraswati, the
supreme teacher, full of brilliance, on Him we meditate.

Offering invocation to the lotus feet of Shri Guru Dev,
I bow down.
Offering a seat to the lotus feet of Shri Guru Dev,
I bow down.

Offering a bath to the lotus feet of Shri Guru Dev,
    I bow down.
Offering a cloth to the lotus feet of Shri Guru Dev,
    I bow down.
Offering sandal paste to the lotus feet of Shri Guru Dev,
    I bow down.
Offering full unbroken rice to the lotus feet of Shri Guru
    Dev, I bow down.
Offering a flower to the lotus feet of Shri Guru Dev,
    I bow down.
Offering incense to the lotus feet of Shri Guru Dev,
    I bow down.
Offering light to the lotus feet of Shri Guru Dev,
    I bow down.
Offering water to the lotus feet of Shri Guru Dev,
    I bow down.
Offering fruit to the lotus feet of Shri Guru Dev,
    I bow down.
Offering water to the lotus feet of Shri Guru Dev,
    I bow down.
Offering betel leaf to the lotus feet of Shri Guru Dev,
    I bow down.
Offering coconut to the lotus feet of Shri Guru Dev,
    I bow down.

Offering camphor flame

White as camphor, the incarnation of kindness, the essence
    of creation garlanded by the Serpent King,
Ever dwelling in the lotus of my heart, Lord Shiva with
    Mother Divine, to Him I bow down.

Offering light to the lotus feet of Shri Guru Dev,
    I bow down.
Offering water to the lotus feet of Shri Guru Dev,
    I bow down.

Offering a handful of flowers

154

Guru is the glory of Brahma, Guru is the glory of Vishnu,
Guru is the glory of the great Lord Shiva, Guru is the
supreme Transcendent personified; therefore to Shri
Guru Dev, adorned by glory, I bow down.

The Unbounded as the endless canopy of the sky, the
Omnipresent in all creation, the sign of That has been
revealed by Him who was That; therefore to Him,
to Shri Guru Dev, I bow down.

Guru Dev, Shri Brahmananda, in the glory of the bliss of
the Absolute, in the glory of transcendental joy, in the
glory of Unity, the very embodiment of knowledge, who
is beyond the universe like the sky, as the goal of "That
thou art" and other (Shrutis which grant eternal Unity
of life.)

The One, the Eternal, the Pure, the Immovable, the Witness
of all intellects, whose status transcends thought, the
Transcendent along with the three gunas, the true
preceptor, to Shri Guru Dev, I bow down.

The blinding darkness of ignorance has been removed by
the application of the ointment of knowledge, the eye of
knowledge has been opened by Him; therefore to Him,
to Shri Guru Dev, I bow down.

Offering a handful of flowers to the lotus feet of Shri Guru
Dev, I bow down.

EXPLANATION OF THE INVOCATION OF THE HOLY TRADITION

The Holy Tradition has been kept alive from time
immemorial. Time has been a factor presenting it in its light,
sometimes dim and sometimes bright, and it is this which
accounts for revivals time after time. The achievements of
the great Masters who are enumerated in the Holy Tradition

have rendered them immortal—not only in the pages of religious history and in spiritual revivals all over the world, but also in the hearts of seekers and enlightened people of every generation. The hearts of seekers, and especially the hearts of those who have attained enlightenment, swell in love for those great Masters and fill with overpowering devotion for them. But for them the light of life would have gone long ago. In the galaxy of such great Masters we find Guru Dev (1869-1953) nearest to us. We cherish his memory and adore him for the great gift of knowledge that he has bestowed upon us.

The entire purpose of the ceremony we are going to describe is to tune ourselves to the source of energy and wisdom from which transcendental meditation stems. There is a set, traditional way of turning our minds to that source. Before we attune ourselves to the Holy Tradition we purify the inner and outer atmosphere.

Apavitrah   —   (that which is impure)
pavitro   —   (that which is pure)
wa   —   (either)
(Either that which is impure or that which is pure)

Sarwa   —   (all)
wasthan   —   (places)
gatopi   —   (permeated)
wa   —   (or)
(Whether full of purities and impurities)

Yahsmaret   —   (he who remembers)
Pundari-
  kaksham   —   (lotus-eyed)
(The lotus-eyed Lord, who is unequalled in beauty, power and grandeur in creation, by remembering him)

Sa   —   (he)
bahya-
  abyantarah —   (outer-inner)

shuchih   —   (purity)
(he gains inner and outer purity)

Apavitrah pavitro wa sarwa wasthan gatopi wa
Yahsmaret Pundari-kaksham sa bahya-abyantarah
    Shuchih

(Whether pure or impure or whether full of purities and
impurities, whosoever remembers the lotus-eyed Lord gains
inner and outer purity.)

We sprinkle a few drops of water.

Then we utter the Invocation of the Holy Tradition. In
this Invocation we repeat the names of all the distinguished
great Masters.

The Lord of Creation has to maintain all levels of
creation—both gross and subtle. Therefore he cannot be
limited to any level of time or space, for the Lord is
omnipresent—the omnipresent level of life is his abode. The
recital of the words helps us to gain Transcendental
Consciousness and establish the eternal truth of gaining
purity in the inner and outer fields of individual life.

Having purified the mind, the body and the atmosphere,
we are worthy and capable of invoking the grace of the Holy
tradition of the great Masters. So we begin with their names:

Narayanam	—	(Lord Narayana)
Padma	—	(lotus)
bhawam	—	(born of)
Padma-bhawam		(born of the lotus)

Lord Narayana, the embodiment of eternal and
Absolute Being, is the first custodian and the eternal
lighthouse of the wisdom of integrated life, from Him it
came on to Brahma, the Creator—Padma-bhawam—who
is born of the lotus rooted in Absolute Being.

157

The truth of Brahma, the Creator, born of the lotus, rooted in the eternal Being, is conventionally and traditionally depicted by a picture where Lord Narayana, lying in a restful pose, has the stem of a lotus emerging from his navel, and Brahma, the Creator, is seated on that lotus. So the wisdom of Transcendental Meditation, or the philosophy of the Absolute knowledge of integrated life came to the lotus-born Brahma from Lord Narayana.

Vashistham	—	(Vashistha)
Shaktim	—	(Shakti)
cha tat putra	—	(to his son)
Parasharam	—	(Parashar)
cha	—	(and)
Vyasam	—	(Vyasa)

From Padma-bhawam, the wisdom was handed on to Vashistha, who transmitted it to Shakti. Shakti gave it to his son, Parashar. Parashar taught the knowledge to Vyasa, the great Veda-Vyasa, as he is called. For it was he who divided the Vedas into four sections, each known as a different Veda. It was Vyasa who wrote the great classic Mahabharat, the central chapter of which forms the Bhagavad Gita. He also wrote the 18 Puranas and Bhagavatam which contains the life history of the Infinite Love Incarnate, the Absolute Bliss Incarnate—Lord Krishna. It is a text book to guide the destiny of, and bring joy to, not only the most abjectly miserable, but also to the most highly evolved Jeevan Muktahs in God Consciousness.

Vyasa's exposition of the Vedic teaching contained in the Upanishads has been the guiding light of intelligent seekers and profound exponents of the truth of all times.

The great strength of the Tradition which renders it useful to all people at all times, whether recluse or householder, is illustrated in Veda-Vyasa's own family. In his life, Vyasa was an example of the way of a householder. His son Shukadeva expressed the integration of life as a recluse. Both these ways of life taken together, make this Holy Tradition of the great exponents of the wisdom of life—a universal teaching invaluable to everyone, regardless of his own mode of living—whether he likes to live in society or out of it. The truth as it is is free from the limitations of any way of life.

So, Parashar, a householder, gave the wisdom to Vyasa, who remained within the fold of the householder's way of living. Vyasa gave it to his son Shukadeva who deserted his home to become a recluse.

Shukam	—	(Shukadeva)
Gauda-padam	—	(Gauda-pada)
mahantam	—	(The great)
Govinda	—	(Govinda)
Yogindra	—	(ruler among the yogis)
mathasya	-	(his)
Shishyam	—	(disciple)

(Shukadeva gave it (the essential teaching) to Gauda-padacharya, who gave it to his disciple Govindacharya.)

Shukadeva gave the traditional wisdom to his disciple, Gauda-padacharya (the great teacher, Gaudapadam Mahantam), who is known as Mahantam, the great. He was a powerful exponent of the essence of Vedic wisdom, Vedanta. His reflections on the Mandukya Upanishad, which is known as Mandukya Karika, are very popular. It is in the Mandukya Karika that Gaudapadacharya expresses the truth that in samadhi the mind becomes expanded and does not contract or shrink, become absorbed or drowned (as is the experience of all practicing transcendental meditation). So, samadhi is the expansion of the mind and not its annihilation.

The great Gaudapadacharya taught to Yogi Govinda the essential teaching of Vedanta, the philosophy of unity of life emerging from the practical field of Transcendental Meditation, which serves to be a direct means of realization of the Divine Unity in day to day life. Yogi Govinda is hailed as Govinda Bhagavad-Pada. Bhagavad-Pada is an expression of adoration. It is natural that when a direct path to enlightenment is received, the source of such knowledge inspires a sense of highest appreciation and glorification from those whose hearts are capable of flowing in such streams of adoration.This is how the seekers and exponents of Vedanta find their hearts satisfied for their expression of gratitude towards the great teacher, Govindacharya.

Yogindra is the adjective of Govinda. It means "Indra" among the Yogis, meaning as eminent as a ruler of the yogis.

Shri Shankaracharya

Such a great, enlightened and fulfilled yogi, Govinda Bhagavad-Pada, was the Master of Shankaracharya, called the Adi-Shankaracharya (the first Shankaracharya) because the successors of his disciples, who take charge of propagating the essential teaching of Vedanta to successive generations, are also called Shankaracharyas. This is to keep alive the memory and the gratitude of the nation towards the first Shankaracharya, who redeemed India from ignorance, which had completely enveloped knowledge and had rendered the nation in the grip of weaknesses and sufferings. The tragedy of knowledge, like the shadow of a man, does not leave any generation.

An answer to such a stitation has already been given by Lord Krishna 5,000 years ago. He says, in the beginning of the fourth chapter of the Bhagavad Gita while recounting the tradition of this knowledge of Yoga, the knowledge of Divine Union, that through the long lapse of time the knowledge is lost. Time is responsible. But there is an eternal factor which distorts the truth of the teaching. What is that? It is the difference in the level of consciousness of the teacher and the taught. The teacher speaks from his level of enlightenment, a level of clear perception and of faultless and precise vision of the reality of life. He speaks to those who are seekers but have not yet attained that level of consciousness. The completeness of expression of the Master, therefore, is naturally received by his pupils in

160

incompleteness. This is what dilutes knowledge increasingly as generations pass; it is the tragedy of knowledge. That is why time, and nothing else, is held responsible for eroding the essentials of the true teachings.

It was the great genius of Adi Shankaracharya which led him to establish in all four corners of India four principal seats of learning for propagation of his teaching, at a time when he had revived the understanding of the people in the country and established the true and eternal principle of Vedic wisdom.

The success of Shankaracharya's work does not lie only in the revival of the understanding of life. He also established a profound system whereby the teaching could be passed on to succeeding generations. Bhagwat Adi-Shankaracharya gave the knowledge to his four disciples:

mathasya	—	(his)
Padma	—	(lotus) Padma-padam
padam	—	(foot)
cha	—	(and)
Hasta-malakam	—	(Hasta-malakam)
cha	—	(and)
shishyam	—	(disciple)
tam	—	(him)
Trotakam	—	(Trotakacharya)
Vartik-kar	—	(the commentator Sureshwacharya)
manyan	—	(and others)

In these lines Shankaracharya's four main disciples are named:

Padma-padam:

The legend goes that Shankaracharya was once to cross a small river with one of his disciples. The boat could take only one, so the ferryman took Shankara alone, leaving the disciple on the bank. While the boat had not yet reached the other bank, the river rose suddenly in a flood. The devotion in the heart of the disciple rose simultaneously, thinking of his duty he hastened into the water. As he stepped in, lotuses

161

appeared on the water under his feet. He crossed the river walking on lotuses which rose and supported his every step as he hurried to reach his Master. When he arrived on the far shore of the river, Shankaracharya called him Padma Padacharya—the lotus-foot teacher.

Hasta-Malakam:

Hasta-Malakam is the name of one of the four disciples of Shankaracharya. The literal meaning of the word Hasta-malakam is "the fruit on the palm of the hand." The ultimate reality of life was as clear to him as an amalak fruit on the palm of one's hand. The expression, which is used for his name, brings to light the clarity of his understanding and the depth of his wisdom.

Vartik-kar:

Sureshwacharya's former name was Mandan-Mishra, a householder rigidly tied to the path of Karma, the School of Karma-Mimansa, the fifth system of Indian philosophy. Shankaracharya had to convince him of the validity of Vedanta, the field of Unity of life beyond the enjoyment of the celestial light of God Consciousness, which is the goal of Karma-Mimansa. Realizing the need for the propagation of the true principles of life, Sureshwa abandoned his home to become a sanyasi. He followed Shankaracharya and being highly learned, wrote on the works of Shankaracharya and travelled all over the country to popularize Shanaracharya's teaching.

Trotakam-Trotakacharya:

Trotakacharya was one of the most outstanding of the four foremost disciples of Shankaracharya. Shankar-charya's air was always thrilling in waves of wisdom through the conversations of the most highly learned and enlightened disciples—Padma-Padam, Hasta-Malakam, and Vartik-kar. Trotakacharya was moving in that air creating pockets of innocence, presenting an ideal of

162

uninvolved witness to the tidal waves of the ocean of wisdom, his heart and mind floating in the Divine radiance of his Master, enjoying the Presence rather than tearing it apart on the scars of logic and discrimination. Not being interested in intellectual pursuits, he was not much appreciated by the other fellow disciples of giant intellect, but the one-pointedness of his heart and mind was actually unmindful of these atmospheric reflections.

These were the days when Shankaracharya was writing his commentaries in his cave at Jyotir Math—one motive dominated Trotakacharya's consciousness, that he should do all that he could so that the Master's time would be saved from organizational matters of day to day living and he might continue to produce maximum of Himself in his commentaries. This was the great act of prudence and timely response of Trotakacharya to the need at the feet of his Master. Being a man of practical approach, he held fast to one thing—service to the Master. He did not participate in the intellectual discussions of the disciples with the Master. Being sincere in his aim he took the duties which would justify his engagement in accordance with his nature—cleaning the floor, cooking meals and washing clothes. This freed the other learned disciples from their domestic duties to give them more time to serve their Master from their intellectual levels.

One day when Shankaracharya arrived at his cave after bathing in the Alakananda River, his three learned disciples accompanied him—but Trotakacharya was left behind. That day it took him an unusually long time to wash his Master's clothes, and so he was late in arriving. In the meantime, the other three disciples were uneasy about the delay in the commencement of Shankaracharya's discourse. Shankaracharya wondered, yet continued to wait for Trotakacharya. Then there arose a whisper: "The Master is waiting for that idiotic disciple who is not interested in the discourse anyway." Just then a melodious voice was heard from far away, thrilling the air and purifying the whole valley of Jyotir Math in praise of the Guru. It was sweet and richly melodious, sung in unheard of and so far unknown meter. There came Trotakacharya singing the praises of his Master in words overflowing with wisdom and heart-rending melody. He had gained instantaneous enlightenment and the most refined state of intellect through the instrumentality of his love for his Master and the reciprocal love of his Master towards him.

Whatever be the shape of the timber, once it comes to the door of a carpenter, he leaves no effort undone to raise its value to the maximum, whatever its quality be. This illustrates that all that is needed on the part of the aspirant is sincerity, unwavering devotion and love for the Master—then spontaneously life gains more and more fulfillment.

Trotakacharya was placed in charge of Jyotir Math. He was the first exponent of Shankaracharya's teachings in Northern India. The other three learned disciples of Shankaracharya occupied seats in three different centres; Govardhan Math, near Puri, Eastern India; Sringeri Math, near Mysore, Southern India; and Dwarka Math, in Dwarka in extreme Western India.

In the tradition of Jyotir Math, the traditional wisdom thrives more on the value of the heart. The rise of the Spiritual Regeneration Movement* for the whole human race is on this cradle of wisdom from the heart.

From my own experience I know that there were hundreds of very learned and capable disciples of Guru Dev, yet the task of spiritually regenerating the whole world fell to one who was like Trotakacharya—and this in spite of the presence of giant intellectuals surrounding Guru Dev. This does not detract from the recognition and appreciation of those of more highly developed intellect, because actually it is they who are more capable of comprehending and

*The original name of the TM® movement, and today one of five organizations making up the movement. R.S.

appreciating more clearly the philosophy and really enjoying the creative application of the whole philosophy in practical life. What is meant here is that even those who are not so highly developed intellectually can innocently be as tools in the hands of the Divine to work out His plan. And this seems to be the tradition in the line of Jyotir Math. Not much learning is needed—just innocent surrender to the Master. This gives us the key to success; we have simple sincere feelings, devotion and sense of service—and then the wisdom dawns. So our tradition of the Spiritual Regeneration Movement came from Trotakacharya, and through time, to Guru Dev.

asmad	—	(our)
Gurun	—	(of the Gurus)
Santata	—	(tradition)
manatosmi	—	(I bow down)

(To the tradition of our Masters, I bow down.)

After naming the four disciples of Shankaracharya, in the last lines, we say —

Shruti	—	(impulse of the Absolute)
Smriti	—	(code of behavior)
Purana-nam	—	(ancient historic records)

The Shrutis are the verses of the Upanishads. They are Divine revelations which constitute the Vedas. The Shrutis were not formulated by anyone, neither by human beings not by any superhuman agency. They are self-expressed Divine expressions exposed to the profound vision of the seers, they bring to light the eternal truths of existence. That is why Shrutis are the ultimate authority, which gives us the wisdom of life, the key to fulfillment of life on all levels.

From these Shrutis, which are the unchallengeable and irrefutable expressions of the Truth, sages have drawn out the codes of life in different fields—individual and social. The codes they prescribed are man-made laws, but entirely based on the authenticity of the Shrutis, bringing to light all the do's and don'ts of behavior. The codes are called Smritis.

The third expression is Purana-nam (of the Puranas). The word Puran means ancient—ancient records of events, covering all fields of intelligent life, from man to angels and gods in the celestial field. Puranas are the history that brings to light the mechanics of nature, the mechanics of the evolution of life. They also serve as historic records of higher evolution kept alive as Indian history.

The Puranas may be said to be a record of the phenomenal phase of the applied value of the eternal truths of the Shrutis, expressed in the Smritis.

Shankaracharya is the abode of all the wisdom of the Shrutis, Smritis, and Puranas. That means he is held in high esteem in his capacity of knowing, and his ability to put the knowledge to practical use for the people, and for that he is also hailed as the abode of kindness.

Alayam	—	(abode)
karuna	—	(kindness)
layam	—	(abode)

(the abode of kindness*)

*Because having knowledge, he applied the wisdom of life to practical living.

Namami	—	(bow down)
Bhagawat	—	(Lord)
Padam		(feet)
Shankaram	—	(Shankaracharya)
loka	—	(world)
Shankaram	—	(emancipator)

(We bow down to the feet of the Lord Shankaracharya, emancipator of the world.)

The knowledge of the transcendental Being so long as it remains theoretical does not help in the day-to-day practical life at all. For it to be of any practical value, some practice is needed to gain experience and substantiate the abstract knowledge. That is why Shankaracharya, having succeeded in making the abstract philosophical knowledge of Eternal Being known, is also hailed as "loka Shankaram."

Shankaram Shankaracharyam
(Redeemer from bondage of ignorance, all negative influences, sufferings or failure in life, bestower of life which has no suffering.)

Why do we call Shankaracharya Redeemer? Because in his theme of revival he brought the knowledge of completeness of life and strengthened every phase of action, thinking and Being. It is the harmony of these three that supplement, support and enrich every phase of life. So, naturally one who brings harmony to all the three aspects of existence is a redeemer.

The theme of Shankaracharya's revival was the same as Lord Krishna's. Lord Krishna also brought the teaching of the integration of the three spheres of life—Being, thinking and action. To lay emphasis on Being, Lord Krishna said to Arjuna in the Gita: "Nistrai Gunyo Bhavarjun" — "Be without the three gunas," and being in this state, free from the three gunas, perform action. "Yoga Stahah Kuru Karmani" — "remain established in Being and act."

So the theme of revival advocated by Lord Krishna was adopted by Shankaracharya and the same doctrine is being adopted by the Spiritual Regeneration Movement to bring the message of Vedanta, which has been misunderstood in terms of renunciation and detachment from the practical field of life. Activity has to be. If Transcendental Consciousness, which is the state of Unity in life, fails to maintain itself during activity, then Unity can never become a living reality in life. The eternal Unity of existence must go hand in hand with the activity of the relative field in order that one may live Unity permanently.

Keshwam	—	(Lord Krishna)
Badarayanam	—	(Veda Vyasa)
Sutra	—	(aphorism)
bhasya	—	(commentary)
kritau	—	(created)
vande	—	(I bow down)

167

(Shankara is hailed as Lord Krishna and Vyasa. We bow down to him, the commentator on the Brahma Sutras.)

The comparison of Shankara with Krishna and Badarayana simultaneously is significant—it is touching and revealing. Krishna, the ocean of the Absolute, finds expression in the waves of the Shrutis*, and Badarayana's Brahma Sutras fathom the heights and depths of these waves. In Shankara we find both the status of Krishna and the wisdom of Badarayana.

Shankaracharya has been hailed as the emancipator or the redeemer also because his teachings have the natural quality of bringing freedom to everyone, irrespective of a person's way of life or condition of living.

Shankara is hailed as Keshawam—Lord Krishna. Another reason why he is compared to Lord Krishna is that, as we have seen, his theme of revival is the same as that of Lord Krishna. In using the term "theme of revival" we suggest that it is not something new being coined or propagated; the same age-old wisdom of the Absolute contained in the Vedic text has been brought out in its pure form once again.

Shankara is hailed as Badarayanam, who is Veda-Vyasa, because by his commentaries he brought to light the real meaning and significance of the Brahma Sutras compiled by Vyasa. What are Brahma Sutras? Brahma means omnipresent and Sutras—aphorisms—the teaching of Brahma, fullness of life, in very concise yet perfect statements. An aphorism is a very short expression but perfect in its meaning.

The Brahma Sutras explain the mechanics of transformation on the path of evolution between the last two

*Shrutis form the basis of the expression of Creation. The Creation has two aspects to it, the relative and the Absolute, and the eternal laws of life expressed in the Shrutis uphold the entire Creation.

milestones of the journey. They present authentic record of experiences to guide the aspirant and support his right experiences as he evolves from God-consciousness to the state of Supreme Knowledge†, which enables Unity of life to be lived as the reality of day-to-day living. The subject of the Brahma Sutras starts from the state of God-consciousness and ranges up to the state of Supreme Knowledge, permanent state of Unity in life. For this end of the teaching the authentic experiences are contained in the Upanishads.*
The Upanishads express and expound the absolute Reality as the ultimate truth of existence, like the sap in a tree which forms the basis of all the different aspects: branches, leaves, flowers and fruit. As the sap is present everywhere in the tree, it can be said that the tree is nothing but sap, and the sap alone is. This is how the Upanishads establish the ultimate, absolute, external existence as the ultimate Reality of all that was, is and will forever continue to be.

†There are seven milestones on the whole path of evolution:
  1. deep sleep state of consciousness
  2. dream state of consciousness
  3. waking state of consciousness
  4. transcendental consciousness
  5. cosmic consciousness
  6. God-consciousness
  7. Supreme Knowledge, in which one lives the Unity of life.

*For their intimate connection with the Upanishads the aim of the Brahma Sutras has been widely understood to be for clarifying the teaching of the Upanishads, whereas the truth is that the Upanishads contain the expressions which formulate the highest level of the teachings of the Brahma Sutras, the supreme level of the whole Vedic wisdom.

The purpose of the Upanishads is to bring the reality of this eternal oneness of life to all men at all times. Whatever the level of consciousness, the teaching of the Upanishads is there to inspire man to live that unboundedness of Eternity even in his day-to-day activities, and to experience joy even during the silence of deep sleep.

It should be remembered that the expression of Reality in the Upanishads is from the level of absolute Existence, because the absolute expression of Truth can only be from the level of Truth itself, the field of pure consciousness, the absolute Being, and for the same reason the understanding of it can only be from that level. This leaves the Shrutis of the Upanishads to be comprehensible and therefore useful only to men already established in Supreme Knowledge. The Brahma Sutras stand by the Shrutis to guide the realized man from the level of God-consciousness to the level of Supreme Knowledge.

For a revival of understanding about life it was vital that Shankara brought to light the Supreme Knowledge which alone leads and maintains man in the highest state of evolution. As this Supreme Knowledge marks the climax of evolution and as this field of knowledge alone can establish thorough coordination between Being, thinking and action, which is the target of revival. Shankara's revival would not have blossomed unless every petal of the flower of knowledge was brought to light. For this reason Shankara wrote commentaries on the Bhagavad Gita, Upanishads and Brahma Sutras.

It is interesting to recall an incident from Shankara's life, when, having completed his commentary on the Brahma Sutras, he was challenged by Vyasa himself on that commentary. From the age of 11 to 16 Shankara lived in Jyotir Math with his four disciples and wrote the commentaries on the Bhagavad Gita, the ten principal Upanishads and the Brahma Sutras. Having completed his work on giving a proper interpretation to these scriptures, Shankara started his journey to the plains to establish his teaching among the people there. When he came near Kedarnath (a place of pilgrimage in the Himalayas) it is said that an old man appeared before him and challenged his comprehension of the Brahma Sutras. Shankara sat down to have a discussion with him and eventually convinced him that all that he had written was nothing but the real intention of Vyasa and that his commentary revealed the true meaning of Vyasa's Brahma Sutras. It is said that the old man was Vyasa himself, appearing to express his joy at Shankara's commentary and to reassure him and give him confidence that the revival would be complete if the true meaning of the Brahma Sutras was conveyed to the people.

The significance of Shankara's commentary on the Brahma Sutras has made him a figure revered by all.

| Bhagawantau | — | (at the feet of the Lord) |
| punah punah | — | (again and again) |

(bow down at the feet of the Lord again and again.)

Yad-dware	—	(at whose door)
nikhila	—	(the whole)
nilimpa	—	(gods)
parishad	—	(assembly)
siddhim	—	(perfection)
vidhatte	—	(implore)
(a)nisham	—	(day and night)

(at whose door the whole galaxy of gods pray for perfection day and night.)

All those desirous of gaining the wisdom of the omnipresent eternal absolute Brahman are true seekers, aspirants for liberation and those desirous of perfection in life.

Shrimat	—	(glorious)
Shri	—	(glory)
lasitam	—	(adorned)

(adorned by immeasurable glory, adorned by glory itself.)

| Jagat Guru | — | (the preceptor of the whole world) |

171

padam	—	(at his feet)
natwatma	—	(having bowed down)
triptim	—	(fulfillment)
gatah	—	(gain)

(Having bowed down to the holy feet of the preceptor of the world, seekers of truth gain fulfillment.)

loka	—	(all society)
agyana	—	(ignorance)
payoda	—	(cloud)
patana	—	(to dispel)
dhuram	—	(skilled)
Shri Shankaram	—	(emancipator)
sharmadam	—	(of very gentle, harmonious and tender qualities)
Brahmananda Saraswatim	—	(name of Guru Dev)
Guruvaram	—	(supreme teacher)
dhya-ya-mi	—	(I meditate on Him)
jyotir mayam	—	(full of brilliance)

(He who is skilled in dispelling the cloud of ignorance of all people, the gentle emancipator, Brahmananda Saraswati, the supreme teacher, full of brilliance, on him we meditate.)

Having recited this and having filled our minds and hearts with the meaning of what we say, we complete the invocation to the great Masters from the beginning of time and fill ourselves with inspiration from their glory. Our hearts are secured in deep devotion, as our minds are held in the meaning of the recitation, hands and eyes engaged in the act of offering.

The invocation through the offerings is symbolic of our universal behavior towards invited and honored guests. Naturally we offer them all the best that we have at home: flowers, fruit, light, bath, shower, towels, napkins, good things to eat, and also we greet them in loving reverence and with sweet words.

So all the ceremony of offerings is significant in the light of the expression of gratitude on a physical level and the whole thing is done in a very natural, innocent and spontaneous manner.

Avahanam	—	(invocation)
samarpayami	—	(I am offering)
Shri Guru	—	(Guru Dev)
charan	—	(feet)
kamalbehyo	—	(beautiful and elevatingly pure as the lotus)
namah	—	(I bow down)

(Offering an invocation to the lotus feet of Shri Guru Dev, I bow down.)

Asanam	—	(seat)

(Offering a seat to the lotus feet of Shri Guru Dev, I bow down.)

A proper delicate etiquette, and in humbleness we offer the seat. The expression of devotion starts with the offering of the seat, because it provides a basis to the action of devotion. The silent demand of this offering of the seat is for permanent establishment of life on that immortal and immovable basis of eternal Being.

Snanam	—	(water for bathing)

(offering a bath to the lotus feet of Shri Guru Dev, I bow down.)

We offer water for bathing or washing the feet of Guru Dev. The silent demand of this offering is for a cosmic bath in eternal Being.

Vastram	—	(cloth)

(Offering a cloth to the lotus feet of Shri Guru Dev, I bow down.)

After washing the feet we offer a cloth for drying. The silent demand of this offering is for the garment of immortal Being, which will forever serve as a permanent armor for protection of life.

Chandanam   —   (sandal paste)

(Offering sandal paste to the lotus feet of Shri
Guru Dev, I bow down.)

Having provided a bath and having cooled the
atmosphere we make an offering of sandal paste to maintain
the coolness. The silent demand of this offering is for the
permanent infusion of that ever-freshening influence of
tranquillity from the Transcendent.

Askhataan   —   (rice, full and unbroken)

(offering full unbroken rice to the lotus feet of Shri
Guru Dev, I bow down.)

When we make an offering of unbroken or full rice, we
make an offering to the fullness of life, heart and mind both
at the same time. The silent demand is for the unbroken
state in the fullness of life.

Pushpam   —   (flower)

(Offering a flower to the lotus feet of Shri
Guru Dev, I bow down.)

Flowers are the expression of the fullness in nature.
There are two aspects to a flower, the outer beauty and the
inner essence or honey. Offering a flower has the
significance of the solicitation for the outer pleasures of life
and also the honey within, the transcendental Bliss. The
silent demand is for gaining 200 percent of life.

Dhupam   —   (incense)

(Offering incense to the lotus feet of Shri
Guru Dev, I bow down.)

Here we offer the sweet fragrance of the incense. This
purifies the atmosphere and creates some pleasantness
within. The offering of incense spreads in the air a silent
demand for inner and outer purity of life.

Deepam   —   (light)

(Offering light to the lotus feet of Shri
Guru Dev, I bow down.)

Ghee flame is the mildest type of flame. This offering is the filing of a petition for the light of wisdom to dispel the darkness of ignorance, the light of absolute consciousness. It is a silent demand for pure consciousness to enable us to have that light of Eternity kindled in our life.

Achmaniyam   —   (water)

(Offering a drop of water to the lotus feet of Shri Guru Dev, I bow down.)

During the offering of the light we may have made the atmosphere warm, so we must cool it again as an apology in case we have unconsciously offended. This is before the offering of food, so that the air will be pleasant and cool. The silent demand is for an eternal basis to the means of maintaining life.

Naivedyam   —   (fruit)

(Offering fruit to the lotus feet of Shri Guru Dev, I bow down.)

This symbolizes the offering of food, presenting a silent demand for a plentiful life.

Achmaniyam   —   (water)

(Offering water to the lotus feet of Shri Guru Dev, I bow down.)

Here we offer water for a drink after the food. The silent demand is for a continuous stream of fulfillment.

Tambulam   —   (betel leaf)

(Offering betel leaf to the lotus feet of Shri Guru Dev, I bow down.)

Here we offer betel leaf* as a means of purification. The silent demand is for achieving and maintaining a state of absolute purity of life in pure awareness.

---

*In India people chew betel leaf after meals in order to purify the mouth.

Shri phalam — (coconut)

(Offering coconut to the lotus feet of Shri
Guru Dev, I bow down.)

The coconut represents the complete fruit presenting the
fullness of life, the unmanifest abstract Absolute and the
manifest field of the three gunas.

The husk (outer covering), the kernel (central portion)
and the milk (inner juice or essence), present the entire field
of the three gunas. This offering is a silent demand for the
completeness of life.

Arartikyam — (camphor flame)

The offering of the light presents a silent demand for
Supreme Knowledge which only results from destruction of
ignorance. While offering the light the presiding deity of
knowledge, the destroyer of ignorance, Lord Shiva, is
upheld in mind and heart.

Camphor burns without smoke and without leaving any
residue. It burns free from any stain or darkness, neither
before nor during nor after. This signifies that celestial light
of pure sattwa which forms the basis and the material for the
world of angels. It is the finest field of creation, yet in the
relative sphere. The silent demand is, "Give us the celestial
field of life to live." Where? In God-consciousness. When
our consciousness is infused by celestial experience, then life
is lived in the light of God. The silent demand is for God-
consciousness. With this as a situation we say:

Karpura	—	(camphor)
gauram	—	(white)
karuna	—	(kindness)
vataram	—	(incarnate)
samsara	—	(world)
saram	—	(essence)
bhuja-gendra	—	(Serpent King)
haram	—	(garland)

sada	—	(always)
vasantam	—	(dwelling)
hridaya	—	(heart)
ara-vinde	—	(in the lotus)
Bhawam	—	(Lord Shiva)
Bhawani	—	(Mother Divine)
sahitam	—	(together)
namami	—	(I bow down)

(White as camphor, the incarnation of kindness, the essence of creation, garlanded by the Serpent King; ever dwelling in the lotus of my heart, Lord Shiva with Mother Divine, to Him, I bow down.)

This verse adores Guru Dev in the glory of Lord Shiva. The role of Guru Dev for the individuals is the same as the role of Lord Shiva for the entire creation.

Lord Shiva has the forces of destruction at His command in order to destroy evil, so that the creation may be maintained in all its purity, and the forces of evolution may work without resistance and the desire of the great Lord may be fulfilled.

Guru Dev has the light of wisdom to destroy the darkness of ignorance and lay open the field of life to purity for highest evolution in the Supreme Knowledge of Unity.

The Serpent King (Bhuja-gendra), who stands as personification of death for everyone, is found as a garland around his (Lord Shiva's) neck. Death not only adores Him but also serves as a means of adornment to Him. As a master of all the force of destruction, even all-devouring death symbolized by the Serpent King adorns his person. He is destroyer of all that is damaging to life.

We bow down to Lord Shiva with Mother Divine, always dwelling in the lotus of our hearts, because the essence of manifested life is duality. Duality can only signify the field of relative life, so when we petition for gaining the Unity of life, we do so to the almighty Lord and his inseparable power which is responsible for duality.

We then offer the light (camphor flame) and after this water to cool the atmosphere again.

Arartikyam samarpayami Shri Guru charan
  kalalebhyo namah

(Offering light (camphor flame) to the lotus feet of Shri Guru Dev, I bow down.)

Achmaniyam samarpayami Shri Guru charan
  kamalebhyo namah

(Offering water to the lotus feet of Shri
Guru Dev, I bow down.)

Pushpanjalim   —   (Offering a handful of
                        flowers)

When we submit a petition for the supreme field of life, it is not made in the abstract. The petition is directed to someone in that sphere of life. Unto Him, the nearest to us in the Holy tradition, unto Guru Dev, we offer a handful of flowers.

Gurur Brahma

Guru* is adorned as Brahma the Creator, because he is the creator of all good. Through knowledge he inspires all good qualities, greatness and eternal life. Through knowledge he inspires creation of balance between experience and understanding, mind and heart.

---

*The Upanishadic criterion of a Guru is a knower of Reality. Both levels of knowledge, experience and understanding, are found fulfilled in him. Being a man of experience he can efficiently guide seekers to gain direct experience of Reality, and being a man of knowledge, well versed in the scriptures, he can easily dispel the doubts of the aspirants and give them a clear intellectual understanding of the highest Reality.

Gurur Vishnur

Guru is adored as Lord Vishnu, the maintainer of creation. Through knowledge he inspires the maintenance of all good in life. Through knowledge he inspires creation of balance between experience and understanding of Reality, which provides a basis to the maintenance of all good.

Gurur Devo Maheshwara

Guru is adored as the great Lord Shiva, the destroyer of ignorance which offers resistance to creation and maintenance of all good. Through knowledge he inspires the destruction of all ignorance which hinders creation and maintenance of all good. Through knowledge he inspires the destruction of imbalance between experience and understanding, and thereby sets the heart and mind to flow in harmony.

Having offered adoration to Guru Dev in the light of the three supreme powers of relative life, devotion rises to adore Him in the light of Brahman the Absolute.

Guruh Sakshat Param Brahma

Guru is adored as Brahman, the ultimate eternal source of all. Through knowledge he inspires the supreme state of life. He inspires the oneness of the relative and the Absolute to become a living reality and brings full inspiration to the spheres of experience and understanding. Both heart and mind flow in perfect harmony and eternal Unity of life.

Tasmai Shri Gurave namah

(To the Supreme, to Shri Guru Dev, I bow.)

Therefore we bow to Shri Guru Dev.

Akhanda	—	(unbounded, unlimited)
mandalakaram	—	(in the form of the canopy of the sky)
vyaptam	—	(pervading)
yena	—	(by whom)

characharam	—	(living and non-living creation)
tat padam	—	(signs of That)
darshitam	—	(having cognized that unbounded eternal Being)
yena	—	(by whom)
tasmai	—	(to Him)
Shri Gurave namah		(I bow to Shri Guru Dev)

(The unbounded as the endless canopy of the sky, the Omnipresent in all creation, the sign of That has been revealed by Him who was That. Therefore to Him, to Shri Guru Dev, I bow down.)

Brahmanandam	—	(Bliss of the Absolute)
param-sukhdam	—	(transcendental joy)
kevalam	—	(alone)
gyanmurtim	—	(the embodiment of pure knowledge)
vishwateetam	—	(beyond the universe)
gagana sadrisham	—	(like the sky)
tatwa-masi	—	("That thou art")
adi	—	(etc.)

(etc. means the other* Shrutis which grant eternal Unity of life.)

lakshyam	—	(the goal of "That thou art" etc.)

"Shri Brahmanandam" — The Bliss of the Absolute. Guru Dev's name — Shri Brahmananda Saraswati is characterized in the meaning of "The Bliss of the Absolute." Guru Dev is adored as Bliss of the Absolute, transcendental joy and embodiment of pure knowledge. Beyond the universe like the sky, as the goal of "That thou art" and other (Shrutis which grant eternal unity).

*Passages like "I am That," "All this is That."

Ekam	—	(The only one)
Nityam	—	(eternal)
vimala(m)	—	(pure)
(m)achalam	—	(immovable)
sarvadhi	—	(intellect of all beings)
saakshi	—	(only witness, nothing
bhutam		but witness, the
		Transcendent)
bhawa-teetam	—	(the status that
		transcends thought,
		the Transcendent)
triguna	—	(three gunas)
sahitam	—	(together)
Sad-Gurum	—	(True Preceptor —
		Shri Guru Dev)
tam	—	(Him)
namami	—	(I bow down)

(The One, the Eternal, the Pure, the Immovable, the Witness of all intellects, whose status transcends thought —The Transcendent along with the three gunas—the true Preceptor, to Shri Guru Dev, I bow down.)

Agyana	—	(ignorance)
timirandhasya	—	(blinding darkness)
gyananjana	—	(ointment of knowledge)
shalakya	—	(stick)
Chakshu	—	(eyes)
runmilitam	—	(opened)
yena	—	(by whom)
tasmai	—	(to Him)
Shri Gurave	—	(Shri Guru Dev)
namah	—	(I bow down)

(The blinding darkness of ignorance has been removed by the application of the ointment of knowledge. The eye of knowledge has been opened by Him, therefore, to Him, to Shri Guru Dev, I bow down.)

Pushpanjalim Samarpayami Shri Guru Charan Kamalebhyo Namah

(Offering a handful of flowers to the lotus feet of Shri Guru Dev, I bow down.)

This invocation and sequence of offerings coming on to us from ancient tradition is dear to us. It is this which inspires us to maintain the purity of the teaching of the great Masters, and to pass on the philosophy of integration of life and the practice of transcendental meditation in its purity and effectiveness, generation after generation. Our aim is sublime, it touches the eternity of time. We want to release the present generation from the grip of suffering and we feel that it is our responsibility to lay a solid foundation for this great teaching to be passed on in its purity to the generations to come. Therefore, it is highly important that whenever we pass on the knowledge of transcendental meditation, which is the key to integration of life, we, as teachers, invoke the Holy Tradition, and in the name of those great Masters of antiquity, we pass this wisdom to others. This is the only way to save the teaching from becoming impure.

If every teacher in every generation continues to impart the knowledge in the name of the cherished Masters of the Holy Tradition, he will naturally pass on the teaching in its purity, as it has been taught to him by his Master. This procedure will naturally serve to keep every teacher in line with the great Masters of the past and his teaching with the pure and eternal teaching of those great Masters.

But for this simple, short ceremony of offering, there would be little in any generation to link the teacher with the Holy Tradition. This would render the teaching only as a teaching from an individual of the present generation, without any basis and security on the road of time. Upon the slightest impurity entering into the teaching its effectiveness will be lost and the whole purpose will be marred.

Therefore, this invocation is the very life of the teacher and the ceremony of offerings forms the body to maintain the spirit of the invocation. It must not be forgotten that this tradition of paying homage to the Masters of the Holy tradition has served and will forever serve to be a means of keeping alive this precious teaching of the integration of life. The act of this traditional invocation and offerings at the time of imparting the knowledge to others is like an act of watering the root of the eternal tree of wisdom.

To understand this more clearly, picture a tree expressing the truth of existence of life, (a tree vibrates the truth of various phases of life). It is there to present its wisdom generation after generation on the corridor of time. It is a big tree with many branches growing in all directions, because the message of life has to be given in all directions, to reach all corners of the earth and to elevate every man, no matter where he may be, and this is to continue generation after generation.

The branches of this tree of knowledge extend on all sides. A branch extending in the eastern direction and another in the western direction—those in the East enjoy the teaching and glorify the eastern branch, while those in the West enjoy the teaching and glorify the branch extending to West. If it were to happen that all those in the East and West, while enjoying the fruits of the teaching, kept on glorifying and singing the praise of the branch feeding them, and forgot to water the main root, then in time to come, the eastern and western branches would begin to show signs of decay and all the branches, old and new, would begin to fade away.

This is precisely the situation of all the different religions in the world today. It is true of every religion without exception. The followers of every religion sincerely adore their religion and are proud in locating points of distinction from others, but the truth of religions is that they represent different branches of the same tree—the tree of knowledge. The same eternal truth of 200 percent of life has been propagated by all religions. How many religions there were and how many of them have passed into oblivion even history seems to have forgotten. How many more will be born in the infinity of time? Each spring gives rise to some new branches of the tree, every age gives rise to new religions. The main trunk of the tree of knowledge naturally continues to support the births of new religions. New branches will emerge but they will be nourished by the same sap issuing forth from the main trunk.

The same truth of life will be broadcast in different names at different times in different lands, but the life of all of them will forever depend upon the strength of the sap coming from the main trunk. If the main trunk is continuously kept watered, the sap of truth will always keep alive branches of religions arising in different times. We have seen how the truth of integration of life is handed on from generation to generation in great clarity, in great completeness, in great simplicity and in a natural way, through this Holy Tradition of Masters. It is this that forms the main trunk of the tree of knowledge from which different religions take their life to guide man from time to time, from generation to generation.

When we invoke the Tradition and make offerings what we are doing is watering the tree of knowledge, watering the main trunk of the truth of life, watering the root of the tree of universal religion, which is responsible for keeping the eternal truth of life alive for all generations, at all times and according to the need of the time manifests in the form of new religions. We feel proud to have been given the privilege to water the main trunk. We rise to bring the truth to every man, no matter what his religion or what his way of life. We water the main trunk and supply nourishment to all the branches. We maintain the universal spirit of all religions on the platform of the Spiritual Regeneration Movement and feel happy over bringing nourishment to the people of all religions, all sects, of all faiths, even though associating ourselves with a particular branch of our own taste. We find our stand is at a point which is universal in character. If you wish to call this universal and eternal tree of knowledge a religion, call it a universal religion to support all religions; if you wish to call it a faith, call it a universal faith to support all faiths; if you wish to call it a sect then call it a universal sect to support all sects.

It may be that someone, seeing us making offerings before a picture, might argue and label us a sect, and thereby try to overshadow the universality of the Spiritual Regeneration Movement, but these formalities, this style of offering, are ways of bowing to Guru Dev or expressing our reverence to the Holy Tradition. These are what we know to be the ties that bind us to the universality and eternity of the integrated state of life, and in order to propagate this universality of integrated consciousness we find ourselves clinging fast to the main trunk. And if in clinging fast to the main trunk someone argues that we are lovers of the trunk as others are the lovers of the branches, we accept their challenge and say: "Yes, we hold ourselves in pride for clinging fast to the trunk which is the source of supplying nourishment to every branch, and if for this purpose we are labelled as a sect or an 'ism' we hail that universal sect, we hail that universal 'ism'."

This is our stand on the spiritual wing of our movement. What are we on the organizational side of our movement? We are an international and universal organization. An organization, even though of universal and international character, has to have some specific rules governing it. Rules and procedures have to be followed, but this rigidity of the organizational set-up is for the purpose of safeguarding the universal character of the precious teaching. These rules and the code of conduct of the organizers of the movement have been framed to maintain the universality of purpose and the faultless maintenance of the universal nature of the movement. Therefore, even though we might appear to some eyes as a rigid organization with many do's and don'ts, we feel proud in binding ourselves to the string of discipline that enables us to hold on to this universal aspect of our purpose and achievement.

There is a proverb in India which says that a thorn (a needle) is needed to remove another thorn. Bondage is needed to come out of bondage. Rigidity is needed to hold on to the unbounded universal flexibility, and thus even on the organizational level of our movement we are rigidly bound in eternal freedom, and with that we are to safeguard the interests of ourselves and those of all our fellow men.

This is the all-embracing universality of the Spiritual Regeneration Movement on the organizational side and on the spiritual side.

Glory to the lotus feet of Shri Guru Dev
the light of the Holy tradition for us.

JAI GURU DEV

Academy of Meditation, Shankaracharya Nagar, Rishikesh, India.

[An eight-page glossary has been omitted. R.S.]

Appendix 3

Excerpts from the Affidavit of
Gregory J. Randolph

The following text is taken from an affidavit by Gregory J. Randolph in the New Jersey Civil Action 76-341, scheduled for trial in late 1976. Randolph's testimony was filed in February, 1976 in support of the Coalition for Religious Integrity, which is challenging the TM® movement to prove in court that Transcendental Meditation is not a religion and a religious exercise.

From October, 1970 to October, 1974, I practiced Transcendental Meditation (TM®) as taught by Maharishi Mahesh Yogi. From January, 1973 to May, 1973, I participated in a teacher-training course which took place in La Antilla, Huelva, Spain. Along with a number of other people, I was personally trained by Maharishi to be an initiator or teacher of TM®. From June, 1973 to October, 1974, I actually taught TM® in Redding, California, and initiated approximately 75 people into the practice of TM®.

One of the most important things I learned from being a TM® initiator is that the whole TM® movement is highly esoteric. There is a definite hierarchy of information; there are progressive levels of initiation, and the farther you go, the more you know. The general public has most of the truth about TM® deliberately concealed from them. The average meditator, who has only achieved the first level of initiation, actually knows very little of what TM® is really about. It's only as a person advances to the level of initiator, or beyond, that he begins to get the teachings on an esoteric level.

For example, when I was learning to be a TM® initiator, Maharishi described the possible states of consciousness as waking, dreaming, sleeping, transcendental consciousness, cosmic consciousness, God consciousness, and unity consciousness. He also spoke very briefly about something he called "Brahman consciousness," which was supposed to be the ultimate development of unity consciousness. However, in the teachings that he gave, Maharishi said specifically that many people in Western society are not ready to hear about the higher levels of consciousness, and therefore, we as teachers should not mention them. He said that we were to teach in terms of cosmic consciousness only and not even talk about the states above it, such as God consciousness and unity consciousness, because people would misunderstand them.

He said that we, as initiators, were only supposed to give out one per cent of the teaching we had received to the people we initiated, so it is obvious that the general public knows even less than that. Maharishi said that he feels that the next few years are critical years for the TM® movement; that, in a couple of years, due to the influence of TM® on the whole society, people will be much readier than they are now to hear about the true spiritual basis of TM®; that he believes that he will soon be able to talk about TM® in terms of spirituality and will not have to talk about it only in terms of science; that he believes this because he thinks we are entering the dawn of the age of enlightenment. In one of his talks, he explained that this age of enlightenment is predicted in the Vedas, the Hindu scriptures. It is known in the Sanskrit language as *sat yuga* or "the age of truth."

There are a lot of esoteric teachings in the TM® movement that neither the general public nor the average meditator ever hears about directly. Another lecture that I recall was given by Maharishi on the subject of how meditators evolve through reincarnation over many life-times into fully enlightened humans and from there into angelic beings. He also commented on those portions of the Upanishads which describe the process of evolution into angels. He frequently taught us from portions of the Vedas, the Upanishads and the Brahma Sutras. Maharishi would also have us begin every lecture session by listening to two Hundu Vedic pundits, who would chant the Vedas in Sanskrit. Most of us had no idea of the meaning of what was being chanted, of course, but Maharishi said that didn't matter. He said it was important to hear the chants at the beginning of each session because the vibrations themselves were holy and would purify the atmosphere and condition our minds to receive his teachings in the proper manner.

I think it is important to realize that, although the average meditator never hears these teachings *directly,* he is *indirectly* being prepared to receive them by the teachings that he does hear. The whole world-view that is constantly being communicated through the teachers to meditators is basically Maharishi's world-view, which is to say that it is basically the Hindu world-view. The language is changed to seem more scientific, but the underlying ideas are the same. It is also important to realize that there is a constant, if subtle, pressure on meditators to "get more involved," to move deeper and deeper into the movement. The meditator is urged to go on weekend retreats, to attend teaching sessions at local TM® centers and to become a "checker." The checker then is urged to become a teacher, and so on. In TM®, one is constantly beckoned toward increasing involvement with the movement and, of course, toward increasing exposure to Maharishi's esoteric religious teachings.

Maharishi also taught us about the mantras during this teacher-training course. The mantra is a secret Sanskrit word which the teacher gives to the meditator at the time of the initiation ceremony. It is the word or sound which is the object or vehicle of meditation in TM®. We were taught to give the definite and deliberate impression to the general public and to individuals we initiated that there are a very large number of mantras and that each meditator receives a mantra which is individually chosen for him and is uniquely suited to his personality. In actual fact, however, each teacher has a list of 16 mantras which are then assigned to meditators on the basis of age classification. The manras were given to us verbally by Maharishi. We never saw them written down in any official version. We were told to take notes on them according to the way they sounded to us in order to memorize them, but after memorizing the list, we were instructed to burn our notes and strew the ashes on the ocean. After that, if we had any questions about the mantras, we were supposed to whisper to Maharishi in private. There was a strict taboo against speaking the mantras aloud . . . .

A major part of our teacher-training was devoted to memorizing the ritual of initiation. There were three separate portions of the ceremony which we were required to memorize. The first was the actual chant or "puja," to be sung in Sanskrit during the ceremony. The second was the physical movements which accompanied the chant, including the placing of the various offerings upon the altar, and the kneeling before the altar at the conclusion of the ceremony. We were taught to kneel and to gesture toward the initiate in such a way as to invite him to kneel along with the teacher. The third was the "puja-feeling." We had to memorize how we were supposed to experience each portion of the ceremony emotionally.

Maharishi said that the performance of the initiation ritual was absolutely essential to making TM® actually work for the meditator, and that was why we, as teachers, had to insist on performing the ritual in a set way and to insist that the initiate bring certain offerings to be used as a part of the ritual. He said that the Sanskrit hymn that is sung in the ceremony had a powerful effect upon the consciousness of both the teacher and the student, just because of the rhythms and the vibrations of the sounds. He said that the puja prepared the soil for the planting of the seed, which is the mantra. Maharishi taught us that the mind of the student must be taken to a subtler level of consciousness through the singing of this hymn so that he will be able to receive the mantra in the proper way.

As a part of our training course, we were each given the official TM® handbook on the initiation ceremony. The book was entitled *The Holy Tradition*, and we were strictly instructed to keep the book itself and all of its contents secret. We were told never to reveal any of the material in the book to anyone and never to discuss it with anyone other than another TM® initiator. The book contains the chant or "puja," which is the main ingredient of the initiation ceremony, both in the Sanskrit version, which we memorized and used, and in English translation (which we did not use or reveal to the initiate), as well as a verse-by-verse commentary on the puja which was designed to reveal its significance to us. The book is unattributed as to authorship, but it was understood by all of us that Maharishi actually wrote it . . .

At the end of my teacher-training course, all of those whom Maharishi had qualified as initiators were required to sign an oath of loyalty to Maharishi, to Guru Dev (Maharishi's dead master) and to the TM® movement in general. At the time I signed the oath, I was in such a state of mental confusion from long hours of meditation that I was only vaguely aware of the significance of the document I was signing . . .

Appendix 4

"Did You Feel Some Quietness, Some Silence?"

Chris Mead

The following article is reprinted from the *Oberlin Alumni Magazine,* March-April 1976, by permission of the author.

Transcendental meditation (TM), with two books about it on bestseller lists in 1975 and over half a million meditators in the U.S. alone, has become a national phenomenon. TM is a "simple, effortless technique," practiced 15 to 20 minutes twice a day, which is reported to promote efficiency and happiness. Its chief exponent is the Indian philosopher Maharishi Mahesh Yogi. Titling my article after a question often used by teachers of transcendental meditation, I hope through a very personal account to give a close look at this movement. — Chris Mead.

As a freshman coming to Oberlin in September of 1972, I believed intensely in transcendental meditation. I had meditated for nearly two years and had checked other people's meditations, attended special courses, received credit from high school for working in Washington, D.C., meditation center, spoken on TM to a number of public and countless private gatherings, and had even tried to "convert" college admissions personnel to TM! I had great hopes for Maharishi's simple technique to work wonders in the world, freeing the human race from stress and allowing all people to find fulfillment, as TM teachings promised.

During the first semester of that freshman year, I looked forward to what seemed an exhilarating, enlightening experience of actually becoming a teacher, or "initiator," of transcendental meditation. For over a year I had saved money from house painting and odd jobs to take care of the $1500 tuition and $220 plane fare to La Antilla, Spain, for five months of teacher training. I was promised by initiators a regimen of increased meditations (up to 12 per day, instead of the usual two) which were to advance me toward what was described as the infinitely fulfilled state of life known as "cosmic consciousness." I would also be able to teach others to meditate, thereby accelerating the world's push toward higher consciousness while aiding my own spiritual evolution as well. All this was to take place between Dec. 31, 1972, and mid-May 1973 while I was on leave of absence from Oberlin College.

Needless to say, I had some doubts as to whether the teacher training course would do all that was promised. I had often had similar doubts about TM itself. The uncertainty, however, only sharpened my need to go to Spain to *find out* the truth, and I hoped thereby to lay to rest my doubts of TM and to allow me to teach the technique with all my energies.

What follows is what I learned, as best I can describe it. I came across the knowledge piece by piece, and only fully appreciated it after the course was over, for it was then, initiators said, that I would experience the complete value of an in-depth acquaintance with transcendental meditation.

The Organization

On Dec. 31, 1972, I arrived on the teacher training course site in La Antilla, Spain. I had expected excellent accommodations and — more important — an excellent organization, for practitioners of transcendental meditation are supposed to be extremely efficient because of TM's removal of many stresses in the nervous system. As it turned out, however, the meditation organization, the Students' International Meditation Society (SIMS), was surprisingly inept. Not only was there no one in La Antilla to give information to newcomers, but there also seemed to be no SIMS people working in town, and there were no provisions for housing, food, or teaching on that first day. I slept that night on a stone floor and on a living room couch for several nights afterward. There were tales of some meditators with rooms, moreover, who wouldn't allow newcomers into those rooms even though the newcomers had nowhere else to go. I was surprised to hear this of people who were supposedly in high states of consciousness.

Systematic teaching did finally get under way about a week after the scheduled December 31 opening. Food was available before that, although one had to stand in long registration lines to get the identification needed to be admitted in the dining room. Generally, the rule for the 20 weeks of my teacher training experience was to be long lines, a clumsy bureaucracy, occasional indifference of SIMS personnel, and poor and often overcrowded accommodations.

At various times during the first week of the course and later on, students were apt to lose their tempers while standing and confronting SIMS personnel. These outbursts were met by SIMS people, and often by fellow students themselves, with some variation of the statement "You're unstressing" — that is, the people who lost their tempers were getting rid of knots or conflicts imbedded in their nervous systems. The theory was that La Antilla, housing up to 2,000 advanced meditators at one time, was an environment of pervasively and contagiously high mental consciousness. The extra meditations only added to this environment. Because of this spiritually refined and relaxed state, the meditators were said to release deep stresses which had previously inhibited their free and dynamic action.

Everyone's hope was that they would lose enough stress to improve their lives dramatically, and this was the promise of the course.

At the same time that people wanted to lose stress, however, they also did not want to be seen losing it in a bad-tempered way — because this was often taken as evidence that they had a *lot* of stress to lose, and were therefore in a primitive level of consciousness. This prevented many complaints, and promoted equanimity in almost everyone. (Some have remarked that U.S. initiators show such equanimity also.) I heard the word "unstressing" used daily during my course experience, and often saw it used by SIMS personnel as a means to avoid otherwise legitimate complaints.

An interesting confrontation did take place, though, before the course was long begun. In one of our huge general meetings several people shouted questions to the course treasurer about how tuition money was being spent. After a number of evasive answers, the audience learned from the course director that all our tuition money was going into the course, but no specifics were given. The matter closed there, because the director, an affable man, had been considered "above" the matter and most of the audience was ashamed to have him have to deal with such pointed accusations. The majority of meditators believed him, and the somewhat abrasive course treasurer served as a harmless focal point for lingering suspicions.

Nevertheless, there were grounds for asking that SIMS course expenditures be made public. There were reports that single rooms in beach houses were being let out for much less than $2 a night (this was the off-season), and most meditators were overcrowded at the time into worse accommodations. Food was known to be extremely cheap, and most of the few services at the course were provided by a small number of meditators who bartered 20 weeks' full-time service for ten weeks' free teacher training. Teaching facilities included little more than five or six color television sets (which were not completely reliable and were owned by

195

SIMS before the course), some microphones, a miniscule teaching staff, and a large blue tent by the sea for our meetings. Since over 2,000 of us during the year were paying over $10 a day for the course, I couldn't help thinking that huge sums of money were left over from costs. Like many others, I felt that part of our money was being used to fuel the rise of TM, and I approved of it, but I also felt we should not have been told our money was purely for tuition if such were perhaps not the case.

Cosmic Consciousness

Our group had not come to Spain, however, to analyze the workings of an organization or to track down financial records. Nearly everyone's desire could be summed up in just two words: cosmic consciousness (c.c.). C.c. was said to be the state of human consciousness which was free from all stress, and which provided infinite joy to the meditator at all times, in the waking, dreaming and sleeping states. People who had reached this state of consciousness were capable of effortless, supremely effective action, "unbounded" happiness, and could not contravene the laws of nature by doing wrong. All that was required to reach c.c. was regular meditation, although certain activities speeded up the process: attendance at longer TM courses such as ours where extra meditations were featured; presence with other meditators (this was a lesser factor); and initiation of new meditators. The initiator course in Spain was therefore clearly an excellent means for us to reach c.c. more quickly, as our teachers told us again and again.

The course membership was very impatient to reach c.c., raising an important and obvious question: how long would it take us to get there? Before I was initiated I was told it took five to eight years for regular meditators to reach cosmic consciousness, and this fact had continually filled me with great hope and excitement. I thought that my experience in Spain would greatly speed up the process, and that I might possibly even reach c.c. there. Once at the teacher training course, I learned differently. I knew one man, for example, who had been initiated before me, who said he had been told it only took four to seven years. On the other hand, some who were initiated after me cited the figure of "about ten years." As initiators in 1973, moreover, we were told not to say how long it took to get to c.c., as it depended on the individual! I began to be nervous about the possibility that some of us might not reach c.c. for a long time. What really disturbed me was a rumor I heard that as more people had been meditating for longer and longer, the time promised for arrival at c.c. had indeed been progressively, tantalizingly hiked up in the following manner: the original timetable for c.c. had been three to five years, which was then raised to four to seven years, then five to eight years, then to ten years, and now was no longer mentioned! The wonderful state of cosmic consciousness began to appear increasingly elusive, and I often worried about it.

Worry about c.c. (in which I was far from alone) could not take away from the excitement which I and everyone felt when our teachers read letters of anonymous students of the course who had actually "popped" into c.c. while the course was progressing. When it came to revealing the identities of people in cosmic consciousness, though, a firm line was drawn. Teachers said that the cosmically consciousness, if identified, would be deluged by curious questions and would have no personal life left while at the course, or perhaps afterward. As initiators, we were instructed, "Don't answer" if we were asked by our pupils whether or not we ourselves were in c.c.

The hidden identities of those in c.c. in Spain only whetted the curiosity of the rest of us, who constantly said things like, "I think he's almost there" or, "She popped into c.c. in the last week she was here." People tried to find in their own dreams, meditations and daily lives evidence of an all-pervasive consciousness which witnessed all things, and which showed them to be approaching c.c. I shared in the excitement for cosmic consciousness, despite misgivings, because the hope of c.c. was a powerful one, and because I was deeply committed to TM. Still, the doubts in me were growing about c.c. and even about TM itself.

TM and Religion

There were said to be two states of consciousness above the near-perfect one of c.c. The second highest was god consciousness (g.c.), later renamed "refined cosmic consciousness." Maharishi said that angels existed permanently at this level, and that mankind through TM could reach it and thereby comprehend the infinity of creation. Higher than g.c. was u.c., unity consciousness, at which level man could know completely the Absolute which gave rise to creation. (In Spain, on one of the last nights of the course, we did actually see a person who Maharishi said had just gone into u.c. The person, named Andy, was an All-American type of nice guy who had sometimes sat at my table for dinner. He read off some of his experiences to a thrilled audience and filled everyone, including myself, with impatience to reach u.c.)

The doctrine of virtual human omniscience through TM, as well as other exciting TM ideas, raised definite religious problems. How, for example, could a Christian accept Maharishi's guarantee of freedom from sin in c.c., or how could people of almost any faith but perhaps Hinduism rely so constantly on a vague Absolute? My roommate was at times quite bothered by TM doctrines' conflict with fundamental Christianity — a conflict which he would be required to deny in introductory lectures. Others, including myself, had also raised questions of this nature. The reply by SIMS personnel for Christians was something like, "Christ said, 'The kingdom of heaven is within.' TM reaches deep into your inner nature and thereby fulfills you." They also said there was no need to believe anything to get TM's effects. It was obvious, though, that that response was not enough. Maharishi's words often conflicted with much of the Bible, Koran and other religious works, and probably even with the *Bhagavad-Gita*, a Hindu religious text which Maharishi tries strainingly to reconcile with TM teaching in *On the Bhagavad-Gita* through repetitive commentary.

In Spain there was only one real confrontation on religious issues. This came when an Israeli woman told Maharishi directly that her religion expressly forbade her to kneel down before images. She was devoted to TM, she said, and wanted very much to be an initiator, but she did not think she could do what every initiator must do to bring a person to TM: i.e., to kneel before a picture of Maharishi's teacher, Guru Dev. She might have added that the recitation of a "puja" which, translated, calls Guru Dev "His Divinity" and invokes other Hindu saints, was also a religiously questionable practice (the puja was to be chanted before initiators kneeled in front of Guru Dev's picture). In any case, after a great deal of excess verbiage, Maharishi said that hundreds of Jewish people had already seen fit to beome initiators, and that it was fine for anyone not to want to kneel before a picture. The only problem, he said, was that those who chose not to kneel could not become initiators! By this time a number of Jewish people felt uncomfortable, and some tried to dissuade Maharishi from his stance. Their efforts were to no avail. Most of the audience was on Maharishi's side, and in any case he had closed the matter.

He was unable, however, to close off the guilt feelings of a number of people, including myself. Kneeling before a picture, chanting praise of saints who were said to be incarnations of the divine, and listening to hours and hours of devoted talks on the Vedas, I felt at times out of place and in the wrong. Most pointedly, I felt guilty for having to tell people that TM conflicted with no religions. While the actual practice of the technique — apart from initiation — had little to do with other faiths, the tantalizing promises we made as initiators were almost equal to guaranteeing divinity to all meditators — or, at the very least, sainthood. Surely this made us a religious group! To deny that was something that was hard for me to consider as an initiator-candidate, but I did consider it in Spain, so great was my devotion to TM. Nevertheless, the technique's conflicts with other religions added to my growing doubts of it.

Disappointment

What finally convinced me that TM was not for me had actually very little to do with TM's religious trappings. It had much more to do with the opposite, with the technique's appeal to empiricism. Before the course I had been told that I would easily be able to see in my daily life the results of five months' immersion in meditation's superior consciousness. During the course, however, my "consciousness" seemed not to have risen but to have fallen hard. Part of a letter to my parents, dated Jan. 21, 1973, stated: "The basic thing is that I seem to have lost (temporarily I hope) that easygoing, pervasive happiness that was building up for the last year or so, and in its place is a fundamental, almost atavistic confusion." The confusion persisted throughout the course, and was at times very painful, but I bore with it because I believed it to be unstressing. Surprisingly, though, after the course (when I was a full initiator), the confusion did not leave. The problem had to do chiefly with doubts of TM and with personal concerns which I had tended until then to ignore — believing TM would solve them at "the root," as was guaranteed again and again.

Despite my troubled state of mind, I continued to meditate regularly for more than six months after the course was over. I kept on waiting for the "unstressing" to end, and for me to feel completely the expanded state of consciousness that was promised me. I asked older initiators what was taking so long, and they said things like, "Maybe you should go to another course," or "Sometimes it takes quite a long time to see how far we really have advanced in consciousness." I listened attentively, but with less and less belief. All I was told, in fact, were things that I myself had once said to meditators in a smaller way, i.e., "You're unstressing," or "Meditate some more."

On account of my doubts I had taught no one TM since becoming an initiator. When in December 1973 I realized finally that my "consciousness" had risen little if any at all since, not just the course in Spain, but even since my initiation in 1970, I decided that TM was no longer something I wanted a part of, and I stopped meditating. I did not even seek academic credits from Oberlin (which I could have obtained) for my experience in Spain.

In Retrospect

Evaluating the teacher training course in Spain, as well as TM itself, is a difficult task. More than two years have passed since I left La Antilla. Considered reflection over that period of time has, however, brought me to the following basic conclusion: that while there were many good people in Spain, there were also many gullible ones — and, more importantly, there were many people whose length of meditation, rank in SIMS' rigid hierarchy, and/or enthusiasm for TM obscured from them some ordinary perceptions of propriety and of right and wrong. Traits such as ignorance, arrogance, complacency, dishonesty and lack of empathy were too frequent among nearly all people associated with TM, but particularly among some high-ranking SIMS aides. The course in Spain suffered greatly from these flaws, and in my mind was unquestionably a failure.

The most severe problem with the course, however, was likely not the people who made it up, but the "product" itself: TM. I do not have the knowledge to back up scientists who dispute TM's physiological efficacy, but I feel I do have the experience to assert that it is probably at best a sometimes-useful tool of relaxation. Those who take an initiator at his word, and believe in cosmic consciousness or even in a significantly and permanently improved daily life through TM, are apt to be quite disappointed. Easily over half of all initiated people have quit meditating regularly, and TM's much-vaunted (and much-twisted, unfortunately) scientific data have yet to identify physiological correlates to that state of being which supposedly incorporates "transcendental consciousness" at all times, cosmic consciousness.

Some may wish to ignore all the higher promises of TM teachers in order solely to find a method of relaxation.

Passing over such things as the disorganization, mis-management, dishonesty, religious associations and other faults which I encountered with TM in Spain, these people will pay $75 or more to see if the technique will give them peace and quiet for a few minutes a day. This is fine, and is their prerogative. They may well be able to answer in the affirmative the question of initiators (asked in slightly different context), "Did you feel some quietness, some silence?"

If, however, the new meditators find the technique doesn't always work, or doesn't seem worth the trouble, or gives them headaches, and they finally decide they would like their money back — and if, moreover, they call their initiator to see about getting the money back — then, certainly, they *will* feel some quietness, some silence!

Appendix 5

The Scientific Case Against TM®

John White

The following article by the author of *Everything You Want to Know About TM* is published here by permission. It first appeared in *National Exchange,* January 1977.

Transcendental Meditation has had such phenomenal success in gaining practitioners because of two factors. The first is subjective reports by meditators themselves—the "word of mouth" method that arises from the enthusiasm of people who feel that significant changes in their lives are taking place due to TM®. These claims may be true and realistic, but they are not unique to TM®. One can and does meet such claims from new followers of any psychological or spiritual self-culture program.

The commonly-accepted procedure here in the West for checking such claims is to apply the scientific method. This is the basis for the second factor behind TM®'s rapid growth. By encouraging scientists to examine TM®, and then using their findings in promotional efforts, TM® has done something that no other overtly spiritual discipline has done. This research has been used by the TM® movement to create a mystique of scientific approval and endorsement. In fact, TM® loudly proclaims nowadays that the world is witnessing the dawn of the Age of Enlightenment, and it is seeing this "through the window of science."

Now, it is true that research into TM® has been an active field. More than 100 laboratories around the world—70 in the U.S. alone—have investigated TM®'s psychophysiological effects and have produced more than 300 reports. TM® attributes this to Maharishi Mahesh Yogi, the founder of TM®, who earned a physics degree in college before he became a Hindu monk. Knowledgeable members of the movement point out that Maharishi's first book, written in 1959, was entitled *The Science of Being and the Art of Living,* and they emphasize the word "science." They also point out that the first research into TM®, which appeared in 1966, was actually performed in 1963, based on Maharishi's call in his book to the scientific community to perform research into the physiology of TM®.

Thus it would appear that more than a decade of scientific research has created an ironclad case for the efficacy and beneficial effects of TM®. This mystique has been instrumental in getting school systems, businesses and even state legislatures to endorse TM® as valuable in just about every area of life.

Recently, however, there have been some scientific reports about TM® which the movement has not seen fit to publicize or even reply to publicly because the results are unfavorable to TM®. This research raises serious questions about both the claims of the TM® movement and also about the quality of research on which those claims are based. Moreover, the movement's response to this research raises doubts about the honesty of its public relations. That is because the rules of science, by which TM® purports to be conducting itself, require that both sides of a question be acknowledged and examined. To do otherwise is to abandon intellectual integrity and the search for truth. If one consciously ignores data to the contrary in promotional efforts based upon scientific research, then what purports to be objective reporting of scientific data is really a distortion of the complete picture that can only be called half-truth or misleading propaganda.

That, in my opinion, is the state of the TM® promotional effort today. Its "true-believer" members are committed to TM® in a fashion that I can only describe as irrational, meaning the abandonment of reason. What other word is there for avoiding public debate and for the deliberate ignor-ance of such findings as the following studies revealed?

In 1973, Dr. Leon Otis of the Stanford Research Institute in Menlo Park, California, performed an experiment "to determine whether unselected, nonpredisposed subjects could learn TM® and derive some of the benefits claimed for it by its adherents and proponents." Another purpose was to test the reliability of earlier reports of significant physiological changes taking place due to the practice of TM®, especially changes relating to psychosomatic problems. Both of these claims were considered in terms of possible self-selection among TM® meditators. That is, Otis wanted to see if the TM® claims really were based on applying TM® to the general population or whether the people who came to TM® and stayed with it were specific types of persons predisposed to get good results.

Otis found that TM® does not alter basic personality characteristics. He concluded that people who feel pretty good about themselves or have few serious problems tend to stay in TM®, whereas those who either already feel positive about themselves or who have serious problems tend to drop out.

There were other findings in the Otis study that also strongly refute TM® claims. For example, Otis concluded that there is some question about the degree to which people who stay in TM® derive benefits from practicing it. TM®

had no discernible effect in changing self-image over a year's time for those people who continued in the SRI experiment. Also, Otis found that claims of improvement in classical psychosomatic symptoms such as frequent headaches, insomnia and fatigue were not time-dependent. A group that had been in TM® only six months or less scored equally improved with a group that had been practicing TM® for more than 18 months. Otis attributed this to placebo effect occurring because the meditator had simply made the decision to seek help in the form of TM® instruction. This, he said, is a well-known situation in psychiatry, where making the decision and taking steps to seek help may be sufficiently therapeutic to the patient in and of itself that he may terminate treatment after only one interview, feeling completely cured and restored.

Otis's report ended with a note about the possible dangers of TM®. He suggested that TM® is a self-paced form of desensitization that also induces profound rest. Desensitization is the psychologist's term for letting repressed problems and feelings come into awareness. Since desensitization may occur, he said, "it would seem that those with insufficient controls to prevent the release of massive uncontrollable anxiety represent a potentially high-risk population for training in TM® . . . without close supervision."

Summing up his position, Otis found that TM® works for some people but is not universally applicable. There are a large number of people for whom TM® is a waste of time, he says. These include both highly anxious people and, at the other end of the scale, those who are already well-integrated. The person for whom he sees TM® as working well is, to use his words, "common in our society—someone reasonably well-integrated, and yet bothered by neurotic anxieties, guilts, and phobias." Many such people are unwilling or unable to take their problems to a psychotherapist. "They could benefit greatly from an easy form of desensitization such as TM®," he said.

Another critic of TM® is Dr. Jonathan Smith of the psychology department at Roosevelt University in Chicago. He prefers to describe himself as a student of meditation who uses the scientific method.

Smith was recently awarded his doctorate for a year-long study involving two experiments to test the efficacy of TM® in reducing anxiety and psychosomatic symptoms of anxiety. He investigated only the psychotherapeutic potential of TM® on highly anxious persons and concluded that TM® does have psychotherapeutic potential. However—and this is a bombshell in TM® research—he found that this potential appears to be due to factors other than the specific TM® meditation exercise. He found that the critical aspects are, first, expectation of relief and, second, a daily regimen of sitting with eyes closed.

Since so many studies describe TM® as a natural and effective cure for mental illness, Smith's research was intended to isolate the aspects of TM® responsible for its anxiety-reducing properties. In his first experiment, 49 people were taught TM® by a local TM® center and 51 were taught a control treatment that Smith himself devised in order to match the content and form of all aspects of TM® indoctrination, including the introductory lectures detailing research and theory, the formal instruction, and follow-up meetings. Particular care was taken to match those aspects of TM® that might foster expectation of relief. Also, the control treatment incorporated a daily exercise similar to TM® except that it involved "simply sitting with eyes closed rather than sitting with eyes closed and meditating." The experiment was double-blind.

The second experiment involved a TM®-like exercise and what Smith called an "anti-meditation" exercise designed to be the near antithesis of meditation in which the subjects sat with eyes closed and actively generated as many positive thoughts as possible. In every other respect, the two treatment exercises were identical.

Both treatments were described to the people involved as an effective means of reducing anxiety, and neither treatment was described as involving meditation. Smith found the results of both experiments to show that TM® was no more effective in reducing anxiety than either of his control treatments. His findings, he said, support the conclusion that the critical therapeutic agent in TM® is something other than the TM® meditation exercise.

Then if the therapeutic effects are not due to TM® meditation, what *is* responsible? As I mentioned, Smith suggested that sitting with eyes closed on a regular basis, accompanied by an expectation of relief, are the true causes.

Smith's assessment of TM® and TM® research doesn't end here. In reviewing the literature prior to his own experiments, he found that most of the TM® studies were faulty. One group of TM® studies were done by mail-in questionnaire. He feels these are virtually meaningless because they are little more than solicited testimonials. "A meditator asked to participate in a study investigating the beneficial effects of meditation," he writes, "might view this as an opportunity to 'step forth for Jesus.' In both cases we are left wondering about those who remained seated." In other words, the people who volunteer to participate in meditation research are probably not representative of the population of all those who learn to meditate, and so any conclusions based on such studies are obviously biased.

Another group of TM® studies tested a sample of meditators before and after learning TM®. Smith found these faulty also because meditators, by their very decision to learn meditation, show some motivation for self-improvement not demonstrated by non-meditators. "Such motivated subjects," he said, "may be ripe for growth and may display reductions in pathology regardless of what they choose to do."

It is important to point out that Otis at SRI found much the same thing as Smith. In his report, Otis suggested that "expectancy plays a critical role in whatever benefits accrue to an individual practicing TM®, and that an important contributor may also be the mere practice of sitting in a relaxed posture."

Recently Dr. William T. Drennan of the psychology department at the University of South Carolina conducted an experiment with TM® to test whether expectation of relief and the regular practice of sitting quietly were actually the key factors in reducing psychosomatic symptoms. Three groups of undergraduates were used—one for control purposes and the other two for experimental purposes. One of the experimental groups was taught a technique described as a relaxation-meditation technique, which consisted of learning to tense and relax muscles from the feet up to the head, followed by a peaceful fantasy with eyes closed. The other experimental group was taught TM® by a local TM® center.

Everyone was tested for change in self-actualization before and after the experiment. The results showed that the TM® group and relaxation-meditation group did not differ significantly in their scores. Drennan concluded that relaxation and placebo-suggestion were uncontrolled variables in *all TM® research to date* except Smith's and that "the unique power of TM® as compared with simple suggestion and relaxation for effecting changes in self-actualization was not demonstrated."

He went on in his report to say, " . . . we would also question the necessity of an individually assigned mantra based on a TM® teacher's mysterious knowledge. Perhaps there is merit in a theory that the use of a subvocal sound synchronizes our functional systems and leads us to inner depths of relaxed awareness. There may be a possibility that a certain sound will work more efficiently for a certain individual than will others. However, until the mystic wisdom of the teacher is open to the scientific public for scrutiny, we can only assess the effects of the practice without understanding."

It was precisely this point that led the psychiatrist-in-chief at the Institute of Living in Hartford, Connecticut to drop TM® from the Institute's research program last fall. The use of TM® in psychotherapy there was highly publicized by the TM® organization during a three-year test period. But when the tests were over, Dr. John Donnelly, the psychiatrist-in-chief, said that the findings did not indicate any significant difference in the treatment of psychiatric disorders. He went on to say that since TM® depends on teaching its practitioners a secret mantra, it violates the ethics of medicine and cannot be tested scientifically by subjecting it to controlled studies. Without proof of its effectiveness, he said, it cannot be considered a treatment.

(In fairness to the TM® movement, it must be pointed out that this decision not to extend data collection was protested vigorously by Dr. Bernard Glueck, the chief researcher there. Glueck said he was just beginning to get data that prove TM®'s usefulness in reducing drug abuse, decreasing depression, anxiety, antisocial behavior and the repressed feelings that cause mental illness.)

The most recent unfavorable research report on TM® appeared in *Science* on 23 January 1976. It was *Science* that first carried Dr. R. Keith Wallace's article about TM® research—the article that first brought TM® research forcibly to public awareness because it concluded that TM® produces a fourth major state of consciousness. Wallace termed it a "wakeful hypometabolic state." By that he meant the meditator was neither sleeping, dreaming nor in normal waking awareness, but rather was in a state that included the deep physical rest of sleep, (i.e., lowered metabolism) within the waking state.

However, that concept was challenged by four researchers at the University of Washington in Seattle. Dr. Robert R. Pagano and his co-workers tested five TM® meditators who all had more than 2.5 years' experience with TM®. Moreover, four of them were TM® teachers. During ten daily sessions, physiological measurements were made, including brainwave studies. During five of the sessions, the meditators meditated in their usual way. During the other five sessions, they were asked to nap, lying down on a bed in a dark room.

The results showed, the researchers wrote in *Science,* that "meditators spent appreciable amounts of time in EEG sleep stages 2, 3 and 4 while they were meditating." Translating that into more conventional terms, it means that the meditators seemed to be asleep, on the average, 40 percent of their meditation time. No significant differences were found for amounts of time spent in sleep as measured by the EEG when meditation and nap sessions were compared. Moreover, in 12 of the 13 meditation sessions in which EEG sleep patterns appeared, the meditators themselves reported that they had been asleep, and in 7 of the 13 sessions during which stage 2 sleep was observed, the meditators said that their meditation had been typical.

Pagano and his fellow researchers concluded that "meditation is an activity that gives rise to quite different states both from day to day and from meditator to meditator." They also suggested that Wallace's concept of a unique, wakeful hypometabolic state is not valid, and that it is still an open question as to whether the beneficial effects reported for meditation are due to sleep occurring during meditation or to some other function of the meditation process.

The public has been subjected to a lot of publicity about the scientific case for TM®. But if the TM® movement sincerely wants to have scientific support, it must abide by the rules of science. This means that *all* evidence from TM® research must be evaluated and responded to, rather than selectively promoting only data that reinforce their own bias. That does not seem to be the case.

For one thing, the International Center for Scientific Research in Los Angeles, which is the clearing house for TM® research and research funding, has an explicit policy of discouraging any comparative studies. That is, the ICSR is not interested in seeing how TM® measures up against results obtained by other systems of psychological or spiritual growth. Such a stance does nothing to enhance the credibility of TM®'s claim to be both unique and the most effective meditational technique, bar none. At the very least, it must be pointed out that this claim is open to challenge since there is no research data indicating anything of the sort. At worst, this claim is a gross example of self-aggrandizement and false advertising.

Beyond that is the matter of evidence contradicting TM®'s claim that the meditational exercise itself is the source of whatever benefits accrue to an individual. Otis, Smith and Drennan point to the expectation of relief plus a daily regimen of sitting as the effective factors in TM®, rather than working with a mantra specially chosen by a trained instructor. If this is so, then TM® meditators have been "taken in" and have paid a high price for "sugar pills."

In addition, Smith and Drennan point to faulty research behind the claims which the TM® movement makes to promote itself. This is a serious charge. Since some of the research has been funded by the TM® organization itself and has been carried out by scientists who practice TM®, there would seem to be reason for considering the possibility of experimenter bias leading to distorted or invalid data. Thus, there is deep need for the scientific community to examine TM® research for soundness of procedures and conclusions.

Should the research prove sound, that would by no means prove TM®'s claim to be unique and unlike any other meditational system. Proof of that would require major research into all other forms of meditation—something that has not been done yet. This lack of comparative investigation into other systems of self-growth means also that TM® cannot claim to be unique on the basis of what it produces in TM® meditators. The benefits of TM® may be equalled or surpassed by other meditational systems, if and when the research is performed. Until then, we simply don't know what science has to say about them. But we *do* know what to say about these particular claims by TM®: they are unproven.

Last of all are TM®'s claims to reveal the nature of enlightenment in terms testable by science. Enlightenment is a much-disputed topic nowadays. From the TM® movement's perspective, enlightenment is the goal of life and TM® is a system—the most efficient, bar none—for delivering enlightenment to everyone on earth. Wallace, who is now president of Maharishi International University in Fairfield, Iowa, published a monograph entitled "The Neurophysiology of Enlightenment" in which he states that TM® is "the most ancient system for the development of consciousness" and that it had been formulated by Maharishi "in a way which makes it fully accessible to modern scientific techniques of investigation."

In Maharishi's model of consciousness, there are seven major states of consciousness. The first three states—waking, sleeping and dreaming—are commonly experienced and understood. Beyond these, however, are higher states of consciousness which are rarely experienced and little understood. The seventh and highest state, unity, is the condition of complete enlightenment. (Lately, Maharishi has revealed in private that there is an eighth major state of consciousness beyond unity, Brahma consciousness, but this is not yet public knowledge.)

To say that all this is accessible to science is a vast claim. It may be so, but the TM® organization has never revealed to the public or scientific community what the physiological, psychological and neurological characteristics of enlightenment are. Nor has Maharishi himself served as a research subject, although he would be the obvious candidate from which to establish these characteristics. Since the qualities inherent to each major state of consciousness are not public knowledge, enlightenment as defined by the TM® is *not* accessible—not yet, at least—to scientific scrutiny.

The TM® movement makes many claims about the nature of enlightenment, but such claims are at present totally without scientific foundation and will continue to be until its esoteric knowledge is made public. The hallmark of scientific validation is predictability. If the TM® organization reveals the characteristics by which it defines various higher states of consciousness, then scientists can follow such criteria in selecting research subjects and in designing experiments to screen out or control nonrelevant factors. Hypotheses can then be formed and tested in proper fashion. If results match predictions, the validity of Maharishi's theoretical construct will be upheld. But until this private information is released to the scientific community, none of TM®'s claims about higher consciousness and enlightenment can be said to have scientific support.

Appendix 6

Who is this man and what does he want?

Spiritual Counterfeits Project, Inc.

Maharishi Mahesh Yogi, as he is known today, was born Mahesh Prasad Warma some 60-70 years ago in India. A member of the *Kshatriya* (warrior) caste by birth, he studied physics at Allahabad University. He later entered a life of spiritual pursuit and took vows as a disciple of Swami Brahmananda Saraswati, or "Guru Dev" (divine teacher) for short. Guru Dev was a recognized leader of the Shankara tradition of Vedantic Hinduism, India's dominant ancient religion. As such, he was one of India's most powerful and revered holy men. Mahesh soon became one of Guru Dev's favorite disciples by means of his unstinting devotion, obedience and service. Through this close relationship he learned the essence of the yoga techniques he later simplified and offered to the world as "Transcendental Meditation" (TM). When Guru Dev died, Mahesh the monk retired to the austere caves of the Himalayas to meditate and commune with "Ultimate Reality." Two years later, he descended from the snowy peaks as a self-proclaimed "master" with the title of *Maharishi* ("Great

Sage") *Mahesh* (family name) *Yogi* (one who has achieved union with God). Banking on his association with the renowned Guru Dev to bring him success, Maharishi put out his shingle as a guru in Southern India. Having met with a rather ho-hum reception in his native land, which is oversupplied with Spiritual Masters, he shrewdly determined to bring his message to the West, whose inhabitants, he said, "are in the habit of accepting things quickly."

Intentions in Disguise

What he *wants* is not so simple and straightforward as who he is. One reason for this is that the TM movement engages in a routine concealment of its nature and a systematic misrepresentation of its purposes. Part of this deception is a strategic response to concrete public-relations problems, but part of it is a reflection of the esotericism which is deeply inherent in Maharishi's tradition of Hindu mysticism.

Maharishi began his teaching in the West as a Hindu holy man, imparting the tradition of the masters in the classical style. However, he eventually encountered two serious obstacles to success: 1) Many secular-minded Westerners viewed "religion" with a combination of boredom and suspicion; 2) Maharishi is firmly convinced of the necessity to teach TM to the masses, as he says, "through the agencies of government,"[1] but because the U.S. Constitution separates the state from religion in all its forms, it was necessary to disguise the religious nature of TM in order to pass it by this Constitutional safeguard.

The Esoteric Gap

This idea of restructing one's outward image with the specific intent to mislead observers smacks of a "Watergate mentality" to most of us, but it is really quite in keeping with Maharishi's brand of mystical religion. This Eastern custom of "esotericism" accepts the appropriateness of a deliberately created gap between the picture that is projected to the general public on the one hand, and the "inner reality"

216

known to "initiates" on the other hand; to say that a movement is "esoteric" is a fancy way of saying that they're not telling the whole truth about themselves. In his *Commentary on the Bhagavad-Gita,* Maharishi reveals that this kind of "heavenly deception" has a scriptural basis: ". . . the Lord [Krishna] warns the enlightened man not to thrust his understanding of life upon the unenlightened . . . the Lord warns the enlightened [i.e., the TM meditator] not to reveal the inner state of their mind to the ignorant [i.e., the non-meditator] . . . He should not tell him about the level of the realized, because it would only confuse him" (material in brackets added for clarification).[2]

This is Maharishi's own description of the "esoteric gap"—a gap that both he and his movement continually exploit in making their advertising pitch to the "ignorant," non-meditating public. Occasionally, however, even the Master lets the truth slip out. At Maharishi's San Francisco press conference, an inquisitive reporter probed an obvious (but all-too-seldom asked) question: "Haven't you been down-playing the spiritual nature of TM in order to attract more businessmen?" Maharishi replied, "I'm not down-playing it. It's only that I'm not talking about it . . ."!

The beans have also been spilled on occasion by lesser members of the TM hierarchy. For example, one world-renowned scholar and expert on religious movements testified in a signed, sworn and notarized affidavit that Mr. Robert Winquist, an official of Maharishi International University (MIU), had openly confessed the deception to him in personal conversation:

 . . . I expressed my opinion that TM definitely seemed to me to be a religion and I wondered why the people in the TM movement denied its religious nature. He replied by affirming that it is certainly true that TM is religious but stated that they did not admit that to be the case for publications reasons.[4]

An even more blatant admission came to light in the course of a public lecture at the Berkeley (California) TM center on July 19, 1975. The Lecturer was Charles Lutes, one of Maharishi's first Western converts. Mr. Lutes currently holds a number of high positions in the TM movement; among other things, he is president of the Spiritual Regeneration Movement (the first organization founded by Maharishi in the U.S.) and a trustee of Maharishi International University. Mr. Lutes told his Berkeley audience that Maharishi has said many people in the West are not yet ready for spiritual concepts and it has therefore been necessary to go through the scientific channels and other channels which are acceptable to the society. It does not matter, in the long run, what reason you have for meditating, Lutes said, because the nature of TM is such that spirituality is the end-result of meditation. Lutes declared that: *"The popularization of the movement in non-spiritual terms was strictly for the purpose of gaining the attention of people who wouldn't have paid the movement much mind if it had been put in spiritual terms."*[5]

The Mystical Roots of Deception

In our opinion, it would be difficult to construe such statements as indicative of anything other than a pattern of consistent and willful fraudulence. Under the circumstances, we are entitled to ask: "what could be the state of mind of those who plot to mislead us so artfully?" The easy answer—and the simplistic one—is to assume that the representatives of the TM movement, from the Maharishi on down, are nothing but bald-faced liars. Unfortunately, the truth of the matter is both more complex and, we believe, more sinister than that.

On our best judgment, what seems to happen is that the minds of those who pursue TM's promise of "higher consciousness" to its fulfillment become so conditioned by the experience of advanced meditation and by Maharishi's teaching about the *significance* of that experience, that they have lost the ability to distinguish between truth and falsehood in the sense that those words convey to the normal intelligence.

218

Maharishi's *Commentary on the Bhagavad-Gita* reveals the profound nature of the process which is at work in TM. As a matter of background information, the *Bhagavad-Gita* is the best-known of the Hindu Scriptures, and tells the story of Arjuna, an ancient hero. Like Maharishi, Arjuna is a member of the warrior caste. This fact means, among other things, that it is his socially recognized duty to fight when he is called upon to do so. In Arjuna's current situation, he is called upon to fight in a war which will decide the succession to the throne of an Indian kingdom. But Arjuna finds himself in a moral quandary, because those he is called upon to fight against are his close relatives—uncles, cousins, etc. They are people he loves and, understandably enough, he does not want to kill them. In the midst of this tension between the call of social duty and the weight of personal morality, the god Krishna appears to Arjuna, ostensibly to act as his charioteer for the up-coming battle, but actually to give him spiritual advice which will enable him to resolve his ethical problems.

In this context, Maharishi's comment is highly revealing: "Arjuna has set himself a task which is impossible unless he attains *a state of consciousness which will justify any action of his* and will allow him even to kill in love, in support of the purpose of evolution" (emphasis added).[6]

Beyond Good and Evil

The "state of consciousness which will justify any action" referred to by Maharishi is, of course, the state to which TM is designed to lead its dedicated practitioners. But it is important to point out that the Yogi is *not* referring to a concept of "the end justifies the means" in the sense that we as Westerners are most likely to understand it. He is *not* saying, for example, that the outcome of the battle is so overwhelmingly important that individual acts of moral transgression, such as killing, assume minor significance in relation to it. What he *is* saying is that from the point of view of the "enlightened" one who attains a state of consciousness which perceives that "All is One," the act of killing has only an illusory reality in the first place. Death only *seems* to occur, and killing is therefore emptied of its moral significance altogether.

Maharishi makes this understanding quite explicit in his further commentary to the effect that:

> The intention here is to bring home to Arjuna the immortality, the never-changing nature of the self, and to make him see clearly that nothing can possibly affect it in any way. One thing was deep-rooted in Arjuna's mind: the feeling that his sharp arrows would pierce and mutilate the bodies of those he held dear and slay them. That is why the Lord begins by making him understand that their existence would not, in the real sense, be destroyed by his weapons. Reality is one, omnipresent, devoid of any duality, without components—that is why It cannot be slain.[7]

The fact of the matter is that both Arjuna and Maharishi succeed in resolving their moral dilemmas by attaining a state of consciousness which dissolves morality. That such is the actual as well as the intended effect of TM's "enlightenment" has been observed by more than one person whose integrity and motivations are not subject to challenge. For example:

> (Maharishi International University) tries to give the impression that it has the endorsement of great minds in scholarship and science, many of whose names are scattered about the catalog. But such is not quite the case. Chemist and Nobel prizewinner Melvin Calvin of the University of California at Berkeley says . . . he considers use of his name in the catalog as coming "perilously close to false advertising."[8]

Mael Melvin of Temple University is another scientist whose endorsement Maharishi once claimed. He has since disassociated himself from the TM movement, saying "Maharishi is flexible in what he considers truth."[9] A disillusioned ex-meditator puts the matter somewhat more bluntly: "Maharishi's conscience has turned to brass."

TM's Gnostic Elite

Lacking any objective basis for ethical decision, the TM movement instead accepts (and offers to the world) the consciousness of Maharishi himself as the standard of personal behavior and the pivot-point of social policy. Maharishi says "All that is good is that which helps the process of evolution. All that we say is bad, helps the soul to go down, opposite to the path of evolution."[10] Since the "process of evolution" is identified in Maharishi's consciousness with the success of TM, the practical impact of this dictum is to make the moral value of all behavior relative to the effect it has on the fortunes of the TM movement!

Anyone can see that such an attitude props Pandora's box wide open. In 1972, Maharishi inaugurated his elaborately prepared "World Plan." It would be naive to believe that this Hindu mystic has dedicated his life to a world crusade to help people relax! Behind such innocently devised trappings is a disciplined, esoteric organization in which spiritual pride, moral pragmatism, power and rigid mind control are all brought to bear upon the final goal of initiating and "enlightening" the whole human race.

The more deeply one probes into the world-view which animates Maharishi's missionary zeal, the clearer it becomes that it is a thoroughly traditional Hindu world-view, replete with political and social attitudes which are elitist and suffocatingly conservative. Agehananda Bharati observes that Maharishi, like most of the "roaming swamis," displays a mentality that is "philistine, uncritical and dormantly Hindu-fascist . . ."[11] Maharishi seems to have combined this "dormantly Hindu-fascist" mentality with the worst elements of Skinnerian psychology and behavior modification to construct a monolithic movement which he runs on the exotic fuel of mystical experience.

We shudder to imagine what such a mixture might mean in practical terms if the TM movement should ever acquire any real political or economic power. Some of the more sinister implications can be seen in a recent statement by one of Maharishi's high level U.S. functionaries:

A study of chickens in which they were allowed to choose their own food showed a difference in ability to choose what was good for them. Some became stronger, larger, healthier and more dominant than others. When the diet selected by the "good choosers" was forced upon the "bad choosers," the bad choosers became healthier and stronger. Thus the good choosers were able to choose better than the bad choosers what was good for the bad choosers themselves! The implications of this for human values and human behavior are enormous.[12]

The Enormities of Enlightenment

"Enormous" is precisely the word! If it does not require much effort for *us* to imagine the enormities which might be inflicted on the world in the name of "higher consciousness," rest assured that TM's officialdom has planned as well as imagined them. One TM initiator confidently predicted that in the day that the "World Plan" achieves its objective of delivering one teacher of TM for every thousand persons on the planet, "all job-applications will feature the question, 'Are you a meditator?' "[13]

Such exertion of economic leverage, however, is only the beginning of TM's ambitions. An ex-meditator tells of his introduction to the movement's *political* aims:

Another thing that really freaked me out was a statement that was made by Jerry Jarvis (president of the TM movement in the U.S.) which I'll never forget. It was made at the Student's International Meditation center at night at an advanced lecture. There were at least 30 people there and I was one of them. I heard this statement very clearly, and I'll never forget it. Jerry told us that . . . since it is illegal for anyone to throw their garbage out into the street because it inconveniences other people, it should also be illegal for individuals to throw their tensions out into society, and therefore everyone should be forced, there should be a law—these were Jarvis's exact words—there should be a law that everyone should have to practice TM.[14]

In case you are inclined to think that this is a grotesque flight of fancy which is personal and peculiar to Mr. Jarvis, attend to Maharishi as he expounds the same subject:

(there is) only one law that is necessary for the governments to make and then every man will be spontaneously law-abiding. And that law would be gain the knowledge of Science of Creative Intelligence and practice Transcendental Meditation twice a day. With this one law, the purpose of all the laws will be fulfilled.[15]

Some Down-to-Earth Questions

This combination of "enlightenment" with totalistic political ambition is a volatile mixture indeed. It has an observably intoxicating effect on those who have wedded their psyches to Maharishi and his movement. As outsiders, however, we are constrained to press some more mundane inquiries. For example: what would the world be like if it were run according to the dictates of "higher consciousness"?

Even though Maharishi has translated the world-view of Vedantic Hinduism into Westernized terminology in order to make TM's ideology more palatable, he has retained all of Hinduism's stifling social perspectives. The implications of this are far-reaching, since the traditional Vendantic response to matters of social rehabilitation is virtually nil. Although Maharishi eagerly appeals for government subsidies to help spread TM under the label of "drug abuse prevention," the organization itself runs absolutely no outreach projects of any sort—all money and energy is directed toward expansion of the movement.

All of this stems from a basic insensitivity to this world and the evils and injustices inherent in it. Maharishi addresses the situation thus: "The answer to every problem is that there is no problem. Let a man perceive this truth and then he is without problems."[16] Maharishi has astutely attempted to defuse criticism of this attitude by expressing the "seven goals of the World Plan" in some fine-sounding rhetoric. Among them, for example, are these objectives: "1) To develop the full potential of the individual . . . 6) To bring fulfillment to the economic aspirations of the individual and society."

But remember the "esoteric gap." What fulfillment of my economic aspirations might mean to the *Maharishi* is not necessarily what it means to *me!* What it *does* mean to Maharishi is clarified by a comment he made in February 1968, at a reception in India which was hosted by the mayor of New Delhi. When asked by a skeptical member of the audience what good TM would bring to the poor of India, Maharishi offered the appalling reply: "They will be hungry but they will be happy."[17]

Maharishi's "Orderly" Society

The brass-tacks question, however, is what stance the TM movement would take toward people who don't want their economic aspirations fulfilled by being made hungry but happy, or who just aren't interested in meditating at all, or—worse yet—who claim that Maharishi's brand of "enlightenment" is really "endarkenment"! Again, we have our answer from the Yogi himself:

There has not been and there will not be a place for the unfit. The fit will lead, and if the unfit are not coming along there is no place for them. In the place where light dominates there is no place for darkness. In the Age of Enlightenment there is no place for ignorant people. The ignorant will be made enlightened by a few orderly, enlightened people moving around. Nature will not allow ignorance to prevail. It just can't. Non-existence of the unfit has been the law of nature.[18]

The mentality of this movement displays every red flag in the textbook of psycho-social pathology: the familiar themes of a-New-Age-is-dawning, follow-our-leader-no-matter-what, we-know-best-for-you, death-is-not-important, and down-with-the-opposition which have consistently adorned the abominations of humanity's political history. Maharishi offers to guide us on another stroll—perhaps the final one—down the path of utopian totalism. Nineteen-Eighty-Four is less than a decade away, but the rule of TM's "philosopher-kings" (to usurp Plato's phrase) would be manipulative, not coercive—except in "extreme cases," of course! Nevertheless, the end result remains precisely the same: control.

Responses and Alternatives

The very existence in our culture of such a phenomenon as TM raises a number of interesting questions. However, if we could focus on a single fact to sum up the insidious character of this movement, we would point to the existence of the "esoteric gap."

The esotericism of TM has two aspects. In the first place there is the simple determination to conceal certain teachings and practices of a religious nature from the public eye. Secondly, there is the attempt (once these teachings and practices have been revealed) to deny their religious character and depict them as statements of "scientific fact" which merely happen to be expressed in religious terminology. Both of these constitute a subversion of the integrity of communication itself. In particular, to claim that affirmations about reality couched in religious language are really scientific in character leads us into a hopeless subjectivism where no objective linguistic standard remains to determine the meaning of anything, or else into a gnostic concept of knowledge, in which only the initiated and enlightened are qualified to interpret reality.

In dealing with this issue of truthfulness versus falsification, we touch fundamental realities and face ultimate moral choices. The truth question is absolute, and primary to everything else in life. Jesus addressed the religious hypocrites of *his* day without mincing words. He declared that their falseness contained the very essence of evil: "You are of your father the devil . . . (who) has nothing to do with the truth because there is no truth in him. When he lies, he speaks according to his own nature, for he is a liar and the father of lies."[19]

Does truth need to be misrepresented in order to compete in the marketplace? Does God need the help of liars in order to be accepted? Compare TM's approach with that of New Testament Christianity as proclaimed by the apostle Paul: "We have renounced disgraceful, underhanded ways; we refuse to practice cunning or tamper with God's word, but by the open statement of the truth we would commend ourselves to every man's conscience in the sigh of God."[20]

When Jesus was on trial before the religio-political establishment which eventually put him to death, he was challenged as to the content of his teaching. His reply illustrates the freedom in candor that righteousness bestows. He said, "I have always spoken openly to the world; I have always taught . . . where all Jews come together; I have said nothing secretly. Why do you ask me? Ask those who have heard me, what I said to them; they know what I said."[21]

What Christ bestows on his disciples is what he himself possessed: the liberty to speak the truth by having nothing to hide!

FOOTNOTES

1. Maharishi Mahesh Yogi, *Science of Being and Art of Living* (Signet edition), p. 300.
2. Maharishi Mahesh Yogi, *On the Bhagavad-Gita: A New Translation and Commentary* (Penguin edition), p. 224.
3. San Francisco *Chronicle,* March 29, 1975.
4. Affidavit of Dr. Robert N. Bellah filed in *Malnak vs. Maharishi,* Civil Action no. C-76-341 in United States District Court for the District of New Jersey.
5. From an "ear-witness account" by a member of the audience.
6. *On the Bhagavad-Gita,* p. 76.
7. *Ibid.,* p. 101.
8. *Science,* March 28, 1975 (Vol. 187), p. 1179.
9. *Ibid., p. 1180*
10. *Meditations of Maharishi Mahesh Yogi* (Bantam Books), p. 33.
11. Agehananda Bharati, *The Light at the Center* (Ross-Erickson), p. 185.
12. Jack Forem (New York Area Coordinator for the TM movement), *Transcendental Meditation* (E.P. Dutton Co.), p. 177.
13. William Gibson, *A Season in Heaven* (Bantam Books), p. 104.
14. Verbal testimony of John Vos, transcribed verbatim from a tape recording.
15. Maharishi Mahesh Yogi, in a television interview transcribed in *The Western TM Reporter,* Summer, 1974, p. 12.
16. *On the Bhagavad-Gita,* p. 66.
17. William Jefferson, *The Story of the Maharishi* (Pocket Books), p. 35.
18. *Inauguaration of the Dawn of the Age of Enlightenment* (MIU Press, 1975), p. 47.
19. John 8:44.
20. II Corinthians 4:2.
21. John 18:20-21.